GWR SIGNAL BOX C

Liveries and Allocations

And other purr-fectly true stories from the steam era

F. E. Line

With grateful thanks to
Peter Barnfield and Bryan Holden

NOODLE BOOKS

© F E Line & Noodle Books 2012

ISBN   978-1-906419-86-8

First published in 2012 by Kevin Robertson
under the **NOODLE BOOKS** imprint
PO Box 279
Corhampton
SOUTHAMPTON
SO32 3ZX

www.noodlebooks.co.uk

Printed in England by the Ian Allan Printing

For more information on Peter Barnfield's excellent artwork, see

www.peterbarnfield.co.uk

A selection of Peter's railway and other drawings may also be found at the

Titfield Thunderbolt Bookshop in Bath.

www.titfield.co.uk

'Behind the Lines' is the copyright of Roseworld Productions Ltd.

www.roseworldproductions.com

Title page - *'THE 'GROSS' STEAM TUG (One Rail Overhead Suspended System)'*

*'A section of the quiet western arm of the Myrtle Canal in Whimshire was used for part of the famous
'GROSS' experiments. By scrounging materials from abandoned jetties at the port of Quill and the remains
of Wittermouth Old Pier, the OROSS company was able to build an inexpensive railway track above the
canal in order to demonstrate its suspended steam tug principle. The wrecking of prototype No 1 after the
collapse of a section of this overhead railway, which also destroyed part of an embankment and emptied
the canal, brought experiments to an untimely end.'*

©*Peter Barnfield*

Introduction

"Signal Box Cats - really? I expect you will be publishing that on 1st April...".

This has been some of the reaction to the idea that a book on this subject was in preparation or might even appear.

Well to prove the critics wrong, I present the following pages - in tangible form. Not in any way to condemn the unbelievers but instead, what I hope, will be a light hearted look at our hobby, both full size and miniature, as well as a look at ourselves.

If I am honest, the history of this particular volume may be traced back over several years. First having enjoyed numerous books on railways, some indeed written in light hearted fashion, various stories from these have remained in the mind. Then having also earned a living by selling books at model shows over more than one decade I became not a little amused by how seriously some of my customers might enquire for a book on sometimes the most obscure topic. This led to me thinking of some spoof titles, which I printed on a list and placed on display.

Those that come to mind included such ideas as, 'A Three Volume History of LMS Dining Car Menus - Vol 1: Starters, Vol 2: Main Courses, Vol 3: Deserts.' Others were 'A History of the Dog Ticket', 'The Wrong Type of Snow / Rain / Wind', 'Hanky-Panky on the Hastings Line', and one final offering, 'LNER Lavatory Pans - Third Class'. The intention was simply to afford some slight amusement, but I will admit I was totally taken aback when someone tried ordering a copy of the last named. (I think he was absolutely serious - so see the next page…...) Whatever, an idea was born.

Years later (and a few books down the road - or should I say track?) I will freely admit it is the ownership and operation of a publishing business that has allowed me the potential to indulge in a whim.

After all, that very publishing business is named after a chicken we once had - 'Noodle'.

Working on the basis that if I don't do it now I never will, I present for amusement, a few ditties and snippets, as well as others by Christopher Burton which are 100% true. Some of the former, where a bit of licence has been taken, may be obvious, some not, I leave the reader to assess which is which. Having also commented on others there is at least one 'taking the Michael' out of myself. Hopefully all may raise the odd smile. Even those where poetic licence has been used have their origins in fact, I will not say where and how, but if like me you have an interest slightly away from the mainstream then hopefully there may be something to entertain in what comes next.

In producing what follows I must also express my gratitude to Alison, Emily, and Richard (perhaps best not to mention surnames here), as well as more formally Alan Cooksey, and for permission to use some of his exquisite whimsical drawings, Peter Barnfield.

I must also express my gratitude to Bryan Holden of Rosewood Productions for permission to reproduce extracts from his 'Behind the Lines' volumes originally penned by Christopher Burton.

Finally, if you do like what follows (my proof reader did advise not to read some pages whilst commuting to Waterloo), I can wholeheartedly recommend, 'Cockles is Convenient' by Bette Meyrick, published in 1981 but at the time of writing, now long out of print. Arguably this has to be the best light-hearted yet totally (railway) accurate story I have ever written. If you do find a copy you will not regret it.

I therefore have pleasure in presenting my own humble attempts, not in any particular order, nor with the intention of any deliberate or inferred swipe at any particular railway. (If you do decide to come looking to complain, I will add we are hoping to move house and take up a false identity shortly!)

Kevin Robertson, Corhampton, 2012.

LNER LAVATORY PANS - 3rd CLASS

Everyone must know the ditty that included the line, 'Oh dear what can the matter be, three old ladies stuck in the lavatory....', but rather than three there is indeed the story of the elderly lady who did indeed get stuck in the lavatory, although not for six days, but it was slightly more than one.

Where – was on the LNER, a company that perhaps features little amongst these pages. When – was in wartime, and how is simply told. For the individual a gruelling experience, but regretfully understandable under the circumstances.

Imagine first the prestige days of the 'Flying Scotsman' in the 1930's. Kings Cross to Edinburgh, in a little over seven hours, restaurant cars, hairdressing salon, and the famous beaver-tail observation car at the rear.

It was on this service that the one character of our tale, Mrs Malone of Dalmeny, a suburb north west of Edinburgh would travel almost weekly to visit her nephew in London. Her habit was to go down on Monday, stay overnight with him Monday through to Thursday before returning north on Friday. Why she had adopted this role was admirable, having witnessed the passing of her sister, her nephew's mother some years before, she had felt it to be her morale duty to care from him ever since – notwithstanding the fact said nephew was in fact almost 30 years of age and although single and living on his own, was well capable himself.

This arrangement had lasted for several years, in truth 'Aunt' Malone probably enjoyed it as much as anything, her own late husband had left her comfortably provided for, the cost of the tickets did not cause any embarrassment although she was also canny, travelling third and not first class.

Come 1938 and then 1939 with storm clouds gathering, Mrs Malone saw no reason to change her pattern of life. Perhaps

it was the stoic attitude that had developed over the years, the belief that having lived through one world war no tin-pot dictator was going to tell her what to do. Hence her journeys continued, albeit at an increasingly slower schedule.

It was on one of these delayed journeys that the circumstances relative to our story began. The train left Edinburgh almost on time, although there was now no hairdressing saloon or observation coach any more, their place taken instead by additional carriages making, if she had known, some 18 vehicles in the train. Reservations were difficult if not impossible at this stage of the war and whilst a timetable existed, everyone reluctantly accepted arrival would be 'when it happened'.

With standing room only even at this stage of the journey, Mrs Malone was well prepared, sandwiches, flask, and a travel rug, plus her suitcase. It was fortunate she was slight of build, the amount of kit accompanying each member of the military almost the equivalent of a second passenger on each occasion.

To the half anticipated accompaniment of slowings and stops, they eventually came to a halt on the outskirts of Newcastle, already well over four hours late and at which stage nature took its course and a trip to the toilet at the end of the carriage became an ever urgent need. Thinking this had better be achieved before arriving at Newcastle station and with it the inevitable influx of ever more passengers and consequent difficulty in moving through the corridor, Mrs Malone excused herself from the compartment, and made her way towards the nearest end of the coach. Unusually the corridor itself was only partly obstructed and so it was easy to access the toilet.

Now fate took a hand, for unbeknown to her the signal had cleared for the train and it was quickly on the move to enter the platform at Newcastle.

Not Edinburgh, nor Newcastle, but the unmistakable environs of Kings Cross in June 1957. The smoky atmosphere is so reminiscent of that wonderful Ealing Comedy 'The Ladykillers' starring Alec Guinness et al. Departing services for the north have been captured by the camera of Norman Simmons.

No sooner had it stopped than there was frantic scramble to get on board by ever more sailors, kitbags, suitcases and equipment thrown in a heap against the toilet door, so that soon not only was the door obstructed but with it the little tell-tale indicator showing 'Engaged'. Outside in the corridor the pile had also reached the ceiling, the owning sailors content to leave their kit in the one place whilst they attempted to find room for themselves in a single compartment.

Despite the notice instructing passengers not to use the train whilst stating in a station, Mrs Malone was not in any position to extricate herself. Within the cubicle she quickly came to the conclusion that to try and open the door whilst there was banging and crashing going on outside would be pointless. What she could not know was that the door was now not only completely hidden from view, but access along the corridor and vestibule was totally impossible, the amount of luggage plus the number of standing passengers meaning progress would be impractical at the very least .

Eventually the noise subsided and she also sensed the train had started to move. She opened the door, to be faced with a canvas mountain. No amount of calling evoked a response whilst trying to push against the jammed mountain of bags was equally futile.

She resigned herself to her fate. A dilemma that would continue all the way to Kings Cross, punctuated unfortunately by numerous further delays, an engine breakdown, and finally an enemy attack on the line ahead, which caused a diversion, reversal, and crawl for several miles.

Arrival was almost 36 hours after departure. It was a tired, thirsty and somewhat dishevelled passenger who eventually alighted on Platform 1, although she was quick to regain her composure.

Just one old lady, not six, just for one day (not six) and in part of a railway carriage about which a certain book title was once consider, 'LNER Lavatory Pans – 3rd Class.'

ENCORE

A good friend of many years standing, Martin Dean, recounts the time he and his wife took a trip on prestige Orient Express. They were enjoying the trip, the scenery, the ambiance of the event when an unknown individual entered what was their carriage. He appeared to be looking for something and was carrying a camera. Not unnaturally Martin enquired if he might assist. The response was, 'I've come from the other carriage but I am looking for your toilet." Martin responded that there was in fact at least one toilet in every carriage: only to be taken aback somewhat by the response, "Oh I know that, it is just that whenever I travel by train I take pictures of the toilets in all the carriages".

(His attire was not commented upon - anorak and duffle-bag perhaps on the Orient Express....?)

'WHITER THAN WHITE - Part 1'

By Alan Cooksey

Evidence given to a train accident Inquiry is not always as complete or as accurate as the Inspecting Officer undertaking the Inquiry needs in order to reach a firm conclusion as to what occurred. Frequently the evidence would become less clear the more witnesses there were to the events. When and where someone took action, particularly if train speed and distances were involved, was often unclear. Although Inspecting Officers Inquiry reports recommended the fitting of on-train recorders following many accidents, it is relatively recently that locomotives and multiple units have been fitted with them. Having information from the recorders greatly assists today's accident investigation, but prior to recorders being fitted Inspecting Officers invented some ingenious ways of attempting to confirm what actually happened….. .

Major Peter Olver, a well-known and respected member of the Inspectorate, in attempting to confirm the evidence given to him by a train driver, arranged for the driver to repeat the journey doing as accurately as he could recall what he had done on the day of the accident. The test run was organised for an evening and, of course, appropriate protection was put in place to ensure that there could be no repeat of the accident.

With the driver at the controls and with Major Olver and a number of senior railway managers armed with a large number of bags of flour the test run train set off. As the driver repeated the various actions he had described in his evidence, a railway manager dropped a bag of flour out of a window. By the time the test run was complete it was too late that evening to walk the route travelled but Major Olver and the railway managers retired to the hotel where they were to stay the night confided that the following morning they would be able to easily identify the big splashes of white flour and obtain a clearer understanding of what had occurred.

Unfortunately even the most ingenious ideas sometimes fail, the following morning Major Olver and the railway managers awoke to discover that during the night……..it had snowed.

'The De-Icing Train, Portesfoote Bunting light Rly., Whimshire. 'Althaea', seen here on a windswept section of the Supia Foliate branch with the morning de-icing train. This equipment was patented by Mr John jacbs of Monkswood Mill, to whom the PBLR is greatly indebted for the idea.'
©Peter Barnfield

'PLUNGER' - The Signal Box Cat

The story of 'Plunger' begins in the last days of steam and ends, sadly, a decade later with the changover form mechanical to multiple aspect signalling.

Throughout her life Plunger was 'allocated' to one particular signal box, the location of which had better remain anonymous, although suffice to say it was on the former GWR main line and also a 'rural posting'. (Certain clues may be revealed from the narrative which follows, but this was not strictly the intention.)

Our story (although 'history' would be a better word, as this is certain fact not fiction), starts around 1960 at what was still a busy break-section signal box. Trains would pass at speed, due to the gradient slightly faster in the down direction than the up but otherwise little had changed for decades. Three regular men operated the box, working the usual shifts, the box being closed from 6.00 am on Sunday until 2.00 pm the same day, thus also coinciding also with the changeover for the night man, who having worked the Saturday night - Sunday morning turn, would go off duty until 2.00 pm the same day.

That particular last night shift had passed without incident, save that is for a deep depression approaching from the west which threatened both rain and strong winds to come. Signalmen as a breed were well versed at anticipating changing weather patterns and in consequence the night man, we shall call him Bill - (not his real name) spend some time sealing the gaps in the ill fitting end-window slides in an attempt to reduce the chance of water ingress. Already the box was in need of structural repair, sixty year old window frames subjected to years of attack from weather and sulphur fumes now rattled as trains passed. The local Inspector had

As if proof were needed, 'Plunger' on an outing to the nearby station - the faded GWR paintwork confirms the location. We suspect he was looking out for the late running 4.15 pm. from Paddington. (He should really have worn a collar marked, 'To work between station and signal-box only'.)

requested many times these repairs be made, but requests like this, as well as to replace a section of threadbare linoleum at the top of the stairs were seemingly ignored. 'Management' had though condescended to provide an electric heater: the fact that there was no mains electricity had evidently not occurred to the accountants, the vain hope of the signalmen for progress in this area was dashed. Mains electricity never was provided. Consequently the working environment would remain oil lit and coal stove heated whilst outside modern diesel locomotives had already begun to oust Swindon green, and copper caps.

Bill's weather prophesy had been correct, just before 2 pm in the face of a westerly gale he parked his bicycle in the locking room and squelched upstairs to the operating floor. After 'opening' to the boxes either side, he passed the first part of shift quietly, at the same time ensuring the fire was well supplied. A lull in traffic came around 7.00 pm, the weather also subsided, bright evening sun casting its rays from the west, almost in mockery against the earlier tempest.

It was then that he first heard the sound, a plaintive cry, a quiet call, unmistakably that of a cat and one which grew louder all the time. Quick investigation revealed a bedraggled and cowering specimen curled up in the corner of the locking room against a pile of old train registers. Apart from being wet it was chilled and offered no resistance as Bill carefully lifted the unfortunate and carried it upstairs to lay it carefully on a cushion in front of the stove. There it remained whilst Bill once more dealt with the passing trains. Each up and down direction move requiring the operation of the respective bells, block instrument, home, starting, advanced starting, and distant signals, plus in the case of the advanced starting signal, a release obtained by pressing the respective brass plunger facing Bill on the front of the block shelf.

G. W. R.

Signal Box Cats
Liveries and Allocations

CHIEF ENGINEER'S OFFICE,
PADDINGTON.

The cat was still sleeping when Bill handed over to his mate at 10.00 pm, Bill would return at 2.00 pm on Monday, armed this time with sustenance not just for him but for the feline. As the days passed so the cat began to recover, food and drink was what was required, together with warmth and security. The men never found where she had come from, nor were enquiries ever made of them to see if a lost cat had been located.

There matters might have rested except that is for the fact that seemingly having watched Bill and his mates, but especially it seemed Bill, the as then still unnamed cat one day took it upon itself to jump from the floor on to the end of the block shelf. Here it sat, unnerved by passing trains or when Bill, tentatively at first because of its position, but necessarily, had recourse to answer the bells and use the instrument to peg 'Line Clear' followed by 'Train on Line'. Neither was it phased by him pressing the release plunger with his duster before pulling No. 35, the advanced starting signal. Instead it just watched, and watched again the next time, and watched again and again.

After this it became a regular occurrence for the cat to jump on to the end of the shelf for most of the Bills shift. Never it transpired with Bill's colleagues, just when Bill was around. Something perhaps to do with the fact that it somehow recognised it was this man who had cared for it all those weeks ago.

Then one day something strange happened. First there was the usual one beat 'Call Attention'. Bill answered in the same way. Then 'Three-pause-One', the code for the 4.55 pm stopping passenger train from Reading. Bill again responded and pegged 'Line Clear'. Shortly afterwards came two further beats for 'Train Entering Section' Bill again answered and with nothing else having passed for some time on the down line was able to 'ask-on' to the box in advance in the same way as he had received the codes. The man ahead gave Bill a 'Line Clear' to allow the starting signal to be cleared and it was then at exactly this point that the cat dropped its left paw from its seated position on the shelf to rest it gently on the button of the brass release plunger for signal No. 35.

The same thing happened the next time a down train passed, then again and again. After that it seemed as if the cat could

sense when it was time for Bill to press the plunger and pull the lever. Never once did it do so for the up line, never did it place its paw on the plunger until 'Line Clear' had been received, and so having told his colleagues who in turn were able to witness it for themselves at shift changeover time, it was agreed by all concerned that hereafter said cat should be christened 'Plunger'.

Plunger was to remain at the same box for years to come, quickly learning it was safe to cross the line to go hunting only when all the levers were 'normal' in the frame (meaning all signals were 'on' and no trains expected). She also became a favourite with Percy the local ganger, who would feed her tit-bits from on the occasions he visited the box.

In appearance Plunger was black, brown and white, all over brown would have been unusual for a cat, but at least there was some connection to the colour scheme of the old company.

No surprisingly she was the subject of much conversation on the 'omnibus' phone during the quiet hours. Questions as to her welfare were common, so much so that on more than one occasion the Divisional Office similarly enquired. It was from this source that information came of the numerous cats that had once been on the payroll of the old GWR. Employed specifically to root out mice and rats when the railway had provender stores and stables. It seemed also that several station masters' had similarly successfully obtained official clearance for a notional sum to be taken from the petty cash each week to supplement the rations of the station cat whose task it was to similarly control vermin locally. Hence the rumour of a ledger that once existed entitled, 'GWR CATS - ALLOCATIONS'. (Another rumour was that within the same office was a book , 'Cats - Liveries & Allocations'.)

On the basis too of the erstwhile belief that GWR policy in various departments had been 'If in doubt add a signal', or 'Add more brass and copper', why should not have been a similar record kept of felines? After all there was a record for almost everything else.

Sadly in the turmoil of modernisation and consequent rationalisation, our particular signal box was destined to be swept away, replaced by impersonal colour lights, unkindly referred to as 'Traffic Lights' by the men and miles of associated concrete troughing. Bill retired around this time, his concern at the time not so much for his paltry pension but more for the fate of 'Plunger'. But again it was as if fate were to take a hand, on the very last day of mechanical working,, Plunger jumped off the shelf down the stairs and was gone. She was never seen again.

The memory of a certain feline in a certain box is therefore only recorded here, as it seems no one, certainly not Bill, ever thought to take a photographic record of his companion in the box - although she was recorded on the nearby station. Likewise if there had once had been an official records of cats on the Paddington payroll, that too seems long gone.

'New Multiple Aspect Signals at Myrtle Junction Portesfoote Bunting Light Railway, Whimshire'.

'Poppy approaching the junction with a train for the Quill branch, which is the line to the left. The installation replaced a number of old disc signals which had become rather overgrown with clematis and convolvulus.'

THE CONVENIENCE OF THE SOMERSET & DORSET

Dr. Algernon Peregrine Thomas Flitly-Smith

Algernon Peregrine Thomas Flitly-Smith was born in Congleton, Cheshire in 1879. Educated at Marlborough and then Oxford, he first studied classics before being drawn to social studies, an attraction it was said, gained from studying the great reformers and leaders of both change and advancement in the 19th century. To this end he became fascinated by the work of Thomas Crapper, later becoming the founder, and possibly the sole member of the 'Thomas Crapper Appreciation Society'.

In studying the social-economic scene of the late 19th and early 20th century and its related demographics, he had recourse to travel the length and breath of the country by train, enduring, according to his notes, many journeys of 'considerable discomfort' caused by the lack of convenience facilities in the third class carriages in which he preferred to travel. (This choice of lowest class transit was in consequence of his wish to observe the working classes.)

One such trip late one night on a stopping train south from Bath, led to such inconvenience that he was forced to alight at Shillingstone in an attempt to avail himself of relief: only to find the door locked and no-one willing to assist. He later penned this rhyme in memory of the occasion;

"On darkest night when south of Bath,
my need became profound...
The toilet door it was locked fast -
just fire-bucket on the ground...."

We may perhaps imagine the rest.

This, he reported, "Let to my desire to investigate the facilities available to the wretched railway passenger at the time." What started then as an interest would turn into an overriding lifelong obsession, eventually covering not only each railway company in the country but also visits to Europe and Persia. Regretfully, not all his notes have survived, those that do however, afford a fascinating insight

into the conditions an intending passenger might be forced to endure.

In Egypt for example, there were communal latrines behind the stations. One of the greatest risks here that of being kicked into the odious contents of the pit by a passing camel. In France it was the traditional 'hole in the ground', enlivened at times by local children, who, on witnessing a stranger venturing to sit, would set light to paper and send this floating down the stream to pass underneath the performing unfortunate.

Drawing by Emily

In Britain too his studies were not without incident. The British obsession with privacy let to his being arrested on well over 100 occasions and charged with such vagaries as "Wilfully openly and lewdly acting in a manner with intent to offend'. He was never convicted, but was bound over on a number of occasions for a common law 'Breach of the Peace.' Few males nor females* it seemed, were prepared to respond to his questionnaire over the comfort, light, facilities, and accessories provided within. In consequence he took recourse in prolonged and repeated visits into the various conveniences himself as well as availing himself of, it was said, copious notes and sketches. (We know also from his diaries that in attempt to access the female toilets he even took to borrowing female clothes. Again the result was arrest.) Notwithstanding this, his pioneering work led to him being granted his doctorate in 1911, although much of the thesis on which this was achieved has unfortunately been lost for generations. (* those females, he reported, that did respond were, he quickly discovered, of a 'unique occupation'.)

But what work of Flitly-Smith that has survived does afford an fascinating insight into the man and his passion. Primarily this covers just one line, the Somerset & Dorset, and charts the full provisions - or lack of, available to passengers and staff on both the main line and its associate branches. As such we learn that at Bath the Ladies toilets, (First class), "...were decorated within in gilded laurel leaf and included seats of polished walnut". At the opposite end of the spectrum, at Templecombe, "Facilities for Ladies were non-existent…"' and "Gentlemen of all classes performed standing only, so exposed to the elements."

Flitly-Smith's notes also afford an insight into the enquiring workings of a mind exercising its talents elsewhere. There is hint of other work, "The effect of Marmite on the spy Mata Hari in WW1", "Can travel in Flying Machines reduce constipation?" and his epic, "Flatulence in the common butterfly - cause and effect", to name but three. We know these works were compiled but appear lost, consequently we will now never know the answers to these conundrums.

What we do know is that his pioneering work on the S & D is unique amongst railways, it can only be hoped that the full draft of his studies may yet one day be unearthed.

TELEPHONES

If you look in the index at the back of Mac Dermot's excellent history of the Great Western Railway, you will not find the word 'telephone' mentioned at all. Perhaps this can be explained by the author's plea in his preface that he was 'wholly unconnected with the railway world'; for, by the years 1927-31 in which the book was published, the telephone was almost as much part of the system as the permanent way.

What is remarkable is how the railwaymen of old who had no telephones could ever have managed at all. How did Mr. Brunel let Mrs. Brunel know that he had been called out and would be late home? Or, for that matter, how did Mrs. Brunel get word to her husband that there was going to be smart company at dinner and would he pick up a bottle of the right stuff on his way home? However did Saunders, Gooch and Brunel manage in October 1842 when Queen Victoria sprang it on them on a Saturday afternoon that she wished to travel by rail for the first time at noon on Monday from Slough to Paddington? And that was a trip that entailed assembling the royal train at Slough, sprucing up Slough station, plus ermine carpets and hussars at Paddington. The poor lad-messengers at Paddington must have been run off their feet.

Presumably in those days they had the speaking tube. It had a whistle stuck into it at one end to attract attention when the caller blew down from the other. But the telephone soon relegated these unhappy contraptions to a role mainly connected with practical joking. A pink and timid junior clerk, fresh from school, would be told that some august personage in the office upstairs wished to speak to him on the tube. Nervously the boy picked up the tube and held it to his ear: a ghostly voice told him to hold on. The next thing he knew was a kettle-full of cold water spouting out into his ear and down his neck, while the laughter of his tormentors in the room above could clearly be heard through the ceiling.

When the railways got down to the serious business of installing telephones, they settled for two sorts. The first was the 'Post Office' or 'National'; the second the 'Bus' or 'Wall' phone.

The 'Post Office' phone was, like its cousins in industry, commerce, and domestic use, both a blessing and a curse. It enabled the public to ring up booking offices to enquire when was the next train to Worcester and, when told, to ask if there wasn't one before that. It was used by vitriolic traders to ask if their goods or parcels had arrived, and, if not, why not? It was even used by suspicious railway wives to find out if their husbands really were on overtime.

On the credit side the 'Post Office' was far quicker and more reliable than the railways' own phones; but it cost money. Thus seekers for information over the phone from other stations or higher offices would use the 'Post Office' as a subtle means to get priority for their enquiries. After listing a mass of preposterous questions to which they required immediate answers, these people would finish by saying 'I'm on the Post Office, so get a move on'. The theory behind this was that the dutiful clerk at the receiving end would pull out all the stops to prevent the company's telephone bill being unduly inflated. Sometimes, but not always.

We had cause to bless the 'Post Office' at Netherton when a crisis arose over George, the level crossing keeper, and his wooden leg. George had lost a leg in an accident some years before, and the Great Western had fixed him up with two wooden legs, one on and one spare. Each year a leg had to be sent to Swindon for servicing and return. It was while this leg was away that a fault developed in the remaining one that he was using. It looked as if he was going to be well and truly "red carded" and we had no one to cover his job.

Regardless of expense, I called Swindon works on the 'Post Office' and asked, admittedly somewhat diffidently, for the wooden leg department. Straight through: no trouble at all. Yes, they said, they would send it off right away. It arrived by passenger train the next morning and all was well.

The company's own 'bus phones were quite another matter. 'Bus' stood for 'omnibus' which meant that the circuit connected everyone of importance in the railway locality to everyone else. The alternative name of 'wall phone' came from the fact that they were usually fixed to the wall at mouth height, with the ear-piece hung on a hook by the side. The user, holding the ear-piece to one ear, stood in front of the mouth-piece and bellowed his remarks into it. Privacy was minimal. A list of ringing codes was supplied in a frame fixed to the wall: so many rings for A so many for B, so many for C, and so on. At the other end you ignored the rings which were not your own code.

Before ringing, the caller was supposed to satisfy himself that the line was clear by listening to the ear-piece and shouting 'Anyone on?' There usually was, and things went like this: -

Caller.　　　"Anyone on?"

First Voice.　　　"... and then I plant them out about nine inches apart with plenty of compost...."

Second Voice. "Ar".

First Voice. "....not too wet, mind, just nice and damp."

Second Voice. "Ar".

Caller. "Get off the line, you two. I want Bristol."

First Voice. "Take no notice. As I was saying..."

Second Voice. "Ar".

One of the most complex of railway telephone networks was in South Wales where many of the circuits created by the little companies before 1921 were still in existence. When ringing up some remote station in the valleys, it was quite easy to get telephonically lost. There was one such station which was so remote that their vital daily statistics often failed to reach Swansea in time to be summarised and sent on to Paddington. This meant that the clerk at Swansea had either to guess them or to ring up. There was still no 'Post Office' phone at this station, and the only 'bus phone was in the signal box which, to make things worse, was on the opposite side of the line to the stationmaster's office. Hoarse, frustrated, but eventually triumphant, the caller would ask the signalman if Mr. Jones, the stationmaster, was there. A stage pause ensued, followed by the sound of a window being opened. The signalman's voice could then be heard loud and clear.

"Mr. Jones," it said, "there's another of those b------s from Swansea. 'e wants to talk to you."

From 'Behind the Lines' by Christopher Burton.

WATER TROUGHS ON THE ISLE OF WIGHT?

The Isle of Wight has an attraction all of its own. Located just a short distance off the mainland of south Hampshire, its limited 30 mile by 15 mile size was once the location of 54 miles of railway. A sad reflection on the changing world we now live means that just 8½ miles retain a public service with a further 5½ miles in preservation, the latter as the wonderful and appropriately named Isle of Wight Steam Railway.

Leaving the last named aside however, and considering for the moment the remaining and now electrified line between Ryde and Shanklin. It is nowadays hard to imagine the days when on a summer weekend this route would see passengers in the hundred - if not thousand, disgorging from the ferry and making their way to board the trains from the Per Head which would carry them through to their eventual destination, usually the coastal resorts of Sandown, Shanklin, and Ventnor. Consequently it was this route, south from Ryde and through to Ventnor that was the busiest. The railway recognised this fact with the line south of Ryde as far as Smallbrook Junction (the point of divergence for the route west to Newport, thence Cowes, and / or Freshwater), operated as two single tracks during the quieter winter months and yet able to be quickly restored to double track operation for the summer timetable, so increasing line capacity and with it the ability to operate the increased summer service with, perhaps slightly more, ease.

Even so, the railway had a difficult time. Availability of pathways, a train taking longer than its allotted time to load, or more usually unload passengers, could throw the whole service into difficulty. The Bembridge, Ventnor West, and Freshwater lines with their limited service were the easiest on which to regain time, but not so between Newport and Smallbrook and certainly not between Ryde and Ventnor.

Notwithstanding this annual problem and the fact that double track on the Island was limited to Ryde to Smallbrook, Brading to Sandown, and the various station crossing loops, the management did for many years operate an 'express' service in both the north - south, and east - west directions. The former was a regular service intended to run from Ryde through to Ventnor, not perhaps strictly 'express' in the recognised term, as it utilised the same locomotives and stock as was available for normal workings, but more a service which omitted certain stops, the intention being that through passengers would be encouraged to use it and so relieve congestion on other services. The other, east - west, train was known as the 'Tourist' and ran cross-country from Ventnor (Town) via Sandown, Newport - where there was of course a necessary reversal, through to Freshwater, not perhaps omitting any stops but certainly the longest single journey it was possible to make on the Island system.

With all of this as a background, it becomes easier to understand what follows and that was a simple desire by the Southern Railway to attempt to run these through / limited-stop services more efficiently by avoiding delays for 'engine requirements'. What these engine requirements were, of course, were necessary water stops, the frequent stop-start and accelerating after slowing down meant the water reserves of the tank engines were quickly depleted and as a result out of course stops occurred - causing even more delays. The answer considered was water-troughs. Not as far fetched as might be thought, as instead of a conventional water trough, the train speed for which would be far too slow, the idea was for a siphon pipe to be placed in a trough and water sucked up using the already fitted Westinghouse pump.

Only a few hundred gallons would be needed and at a speed of between perhaps 10 - 20 mph, the length of trough would be set at a quarter of a mile, which distance would be covered. in 45 seconds at 20 mph. The other technical issue so far as the locomotive and the raising of water was concerned, was the simple addition of a lever within the cab which, when operated, would both lower a pipe having an open chute at either end into the trough as well as commencing the Westinghouse pump operation. It is rumoured one engine may have been experimentally fitted and successfully raised water on a static basis from a tin bath placed underneath the pipe. Regretfully no photographs have survived.

But the next stage was where to locate the troughs, and for this much care had to be exercised. Basically the requirements were identical to that of conventional, higher speed (mainland), trough operation. Bearing in mind the Southern had no experience of this working it was a definite step into the unknown. Fortunately all three other companies appeared content to pool (- no pun intended) their knowledge, with advice reference the necessary quality of water at the chosen site(s), the essential pre-requite of level track, no underbridges in the vicinity, and a recognition that sleepers and formation in the selected area would need to be the subject of greater maintenance. There was also the cost of the actual equipment as well as a water storage tank and pumping

equipment at the chosen site to maintain the required level of water in the trough. All these 'static' costs were then added together being including the cost of locomotive equipment fitment -and maintenance. To balance the case was the advantage to be gained, greater flexibility in operation and improved train timekeeping.

It appears the Southern Railway seriously considered three actual locations. The first two were on the route of the 'Tourist', between Alverstone and Newchurch, the third west of Newport a short distance east of Yarmouth station. Elsewhere on the train's route there was little in the way of level track. On the main line, if we may call it as such, the situation was similarly less than ideal and it was for these reasons that the it appears the idea may not have been proceeded with.

Around this time, the 'mechanicals', meaning the locomotive department came up with another potential

stumbling block. The Westinghouse pump would normally operate automatically when required: to maintain air pressure in the reservoir. If it was in the actual process of working when it was needed for pumping water, and if the engine reservoir had a leak or there was a leak in the system elsewhere, then the process of switching from pumping air to pumping water could result in the train brakes being applied. Under conditions of normal maintenance this should not occur, but we all know the railways often operated in a less than ideal condition. Another issue then to consider and weight-up as a disadvantage. Perhaps more surprisingly the thought of water being pumped through into the air reservoir or high pressure air being forced into the water tanks does not seem to have been considered.

Possibly the simplest all-round solution would have been a tank wagon coupled immediately behind the locomotive, obvious perhaps but instead it seems someone wanted to look for the more complicated solution.

PULLMAN on the LISTOWEL & BALLYBUNION

If ever there was a railway in the mould of W Heath-Robinson it must have been the Listowel & Ballybunion. Perhaps it is even incorrect to refer to it as a railway, monorail may be more correct - whatever, and with every deference to the people of that wonderful country, Ireland, it must surely have been one of the strangest means of 'railway' transport ever devised.

In case there is anyone not perhaps familiar with this wonderful system a quote from the website http://www.lartiguemonorail.com/Page%202.htm affords a concise history:

"The monorail employed on the Listowel-Ballybunion line was invented and developed by a French Engineer by the name of Charles Lartigue, hence the name Lartigue Monorailway by which the line was best known. Lartigue had built a prototype monorail in Algeria, it was about 90Km in length and was used to carry esparto grass across the desert. The cargo was carried in pannier-like wagons slung on either side of a single rail, which was itself mounted on A-shaped trestles. The wagons were connected to bogies whose wheels ran along the rail. Lartigue is reputed to have got the inspiration for this design from watching camels serenely carrying large loads in panniers balanced either side of their backs. There is no doubt that the single raised rail was a distinct advantage in the desert where shifting sands would have made a conventional rail line virtually unusable.

" In 1886 Lartigue brought a length of his line to an exhibition in London in the hope of selling his idea as a viable railway option. Coincidentally at this time the populace of North Kerry were lobbying for the railway system to be extended to include a link between Listowel and Ballybunion. This request was at that time lying on a minister's desk in Westminster, the rest as they say is history. It was decided that the Lartigue system would be tried out on the Listowel-Ballybunion Railway.

"The Listowel-Ballybunion Railway was opened in 1888 at a cost of £30,000 and ran for 36 years until closed in 1924.

The closure was hastened by severe damage inflicted on the line during the civil war of 1921-23. The line was only barely financially viable for the whole of its existence, it is reputed never to have made a profit. The train carried freight, cattle, sand from the beaches and passengers. Among the passengers were Ballybunion school children going to the Listowel Secondary Schools, Kerry and Limerick people making their way to the beach resort of Ballybunion and golfers going to the fledgling golf course at Ballybunion which was to develop into one of the greatest golf courses in the world."

There the formal history might end, suffice to say the 'pannier' idea had, of course, been taken up quite independently by Swindon so far as their 0-6-0T engine designs were concerned. Here the ability to have raised water tanks enabled far easier access to the inside motion, the water tanks themselves connected by a balancing pipe. (It is rumoured Stanier, when he left Swindon for Crewe took with him the idea for a pannier tank design for the LMS. As it was there was never a need for a modern 0-6-0T design from Crewe or Derby and as such the tank engines types that were built by the LMS were of larger 2-6-2T or 2-6-4T type and so recognised as unsuitable for the panniers.)

But to return to the Lartigue, there is the persistent story of the cow that was required to be transported from one end of the line to the other but in so doing it was recognised that the weight of the beast would be totally unsuitable if carried on one side of the monorail. Consequently the decision was made to effect a balance by loading the beast on one side with a counterbalance in the form of two calves on the opposite side. The latter were there solely for the ride - so to speak - as at the destination the adult animal was unloaded and one calf walked around to take its place. As such equilibrium was restored for the return journey. Care was no doubt similarly exercised when loading shoppers and other goods, as such passengers might not always have had the opportunity to sit where they would always wish.

This quaint (the word is used with the greatest respect) system attracted attention from engineers far and wide although as far as is known, whilst sympathetic and appreciative of the principals and advantages, no other 'railway' was built to the same concept. (In 1930 George Bennie built a short test monorail at Milngavie, Glasgow, and where he demonstrated a propeller driver vehicle carried underneath an 'A' frame.)

One of the men supposedly intrigued by the Lartigue was not as perhaps might be thought, Holman Stevens, but George Mortimer Pullman. The Pullman brand of luxury rail travel had already arrived in England and no doubt with the aim of expanding further he was ever on the lookout for opportunity.

The Line between Listowel and Ballybunion might then seem an unlikely candidate, but research at the public bar of a certain brewery in Dublin revealed there were a number of wealthy landowners in the area at the time - some revered by their tenants - other equally despised. Whatever, the company evidently felt they might indeed embrace a luxury travel, with a literal balance between the sides of the cars created by having an individual steward per passenger.

In theory this was an excellent attempt to effect a balance, the only problem came when the relative proportions of the passenger and steward were taken into account. An unequal weight distribution followed which increased still further as the passenger imbibed and partook of the various offerings available. The result was an unbalanced car quickly creating a nauseous effect. The experiment was quickly abandoned.

Suffice to say that in England Mr Bulleid had attempted to override the laws of physics with his offset boiler on the 'Leader'. The resultant unequal weight distribution meaning pig iron had to be added to achieve a more equal weight distribution. We have of course mentioned Mr Bulleid in the past, remember too that after finishing with the Southern Railway he eventually took up his final engineering post in Dublin. Perhaps with his coming the wheel had indeed gone full circle.

©Peter Barnfield

TRAGEDY and EXTRA REVENUE

The tunnel at Combe Down on the lamented Somerset & Dorset south of Bath has had its far share of notoriety. For 92 years steam hauled trains would make their way through the 1,829 yard edifice which had the unenviable distinction of the longest single bore tunnel on a UK railway without any form of intermediate ventilation.

Nearly half a century since the final trains ran, the route has, or is planned, to be reopened - not sadly as a revised railway (too much of the remainder of the S & D route has been lost so making any attempt to re-establish a line between Bath and Bournemouth little more than a dream, but instead as a cycle path, aided by a modern day cycle-friendly surface, mobile phone coverage and lighting linked to motion sensors. Previously since the demise of the railway the tunnel has for many years been the home to a number of bat colonies.

In steam days the task of the taking a train through the tunnel was no easy task. Modern steam locomotives were built to the very limits of the available loading gauge, meaning the space between the top of the chimney and tunnel roof was measured in inches - and not many of those - thus smoke and steam would beat down, to quickly envelope those on the footplate in a sulphurous fog, making breathing and sight increasingly difficult.

Such conditions had been tolerated from 1874 onwards and similarly there were several close-shaves with a crew almost overcome by an atmosphere which could become unbreathable. This is indeed what did happen on 20 November 1929, the driver and fireman of a northbound goods train being overcome by the fumes. The train, 32 wagons of coal and six other wagons including a brake van weighed 493 tons, was moving very slowly in the tunnel due to the heavy load, not helped by having been brought to a standstill at the last station before the tunnel: Midford. The engine, 2-8-0 No. 89 was also running tender first which might have been expected to have afforded some relieve to the crew, but it was later established that the slow speed of the train allied to exceptional humidity of the day in question even if the ambient temperature was not excessive,

plus the lack of any form of breeze, were to cause disaster. Both the driver and fireman were overcome within the tunnel. Fireman Pearce, who survived recalled the atmosphere was very hot within causing him to cough violently. He then wrapped his coat around his head and sat down. At this point the driver was still at the controls, but shortly afterwards Pearce must have passed out

At the rear of the train the guard was aware the train was moving very slowly, he admitted later he had to shine his lamp at the tunnel wall to see if they were actually moving forward. On breasting the summit the engine still had steam applied and it was in this state that it now continued at ever increasing speed. We may only imagine the conditions the crew had endured, but with neither conscious the engine breasted the summit of the climb - located within the tunnel - and commenced a headlong dash to destruction in the goods yard at Bath almost three miles further on.

Driver Jennings was extricated from the wreck alive, but only just, he died on his way to hospital. Fireman Pearce survived but not so two other railwayman in the yard itself who were killed by debris.

Where is this leading, well simply to say that any attempt at frivolity after what is a totally true and tragic case might rightly be seen as extreme bad taste. Suffice it to say that like all other railway companies, the Somerset & Dorset had also attempted to accrue additional revenue from any source it could. This would include the obvious transport of goods, but they also achieved some success though selling space for advertising on its fixed structures, allowing space for vending machines and of course lineside space for allotments - the last named usually leased to members of staff for a peppercorn sum but with the bonus that the boundaries of the railway were thus tendered and watched. Additionally, the S & D although possibly not unique in this context but this cannot be confirmed, was reported as collecting soot from the inside of the Combe Down tunnel in the early years of its existence which when mixed with salt formed an early type of toothpaste. (Some people were still using such a concoction on their teeth in the 1950s.)

Of course in the days when the use of coal was far more prevalent than it is today so then were supplies of soot, whilst as coal began to decline so did the need for soot. What was left hanging from the walls and roof of Combe Down tunnel in 1966 after the last train had passed was probably an accumulation of soot from perhaps the last 60 years at least. Intermingled somewhere in this is no doubt the vestige of coal burnt by No. 89 on that fateful day.

To a modern day generation the very thought of using such remedies for hygiene purposes is unthinkable, but in other respects sometimes the wheel may turn full circle to what it was many years ago. In this context there are reports that in the years immediately following the turn of the 20th century, the independent north-south line, the Midland & South Western Junction, had a regular traffic in dog droppings which it carried in barrels from Andover to Weyhill for disposal. This traffic ceased, possibly because such unpleasant deposits whilst initially tolerated were finally unwelcome.

A century later as a society we now demand any such deposits are collected and similarly taken away. But as with the S & D and its sales of soot, not by train to Weyhill, but instead by poopa-scooper and hygienic bag.

©Peter Barnfield

MEETINGS FOR STATION MASTERS' AND GOODS AGENTS' ON THE GWR

If you looked hard enough at Paddington in the archives for about 1840, I am sure you would find a record of the first station masters' meeting The line had been opened as far as Reading and it is easy to picture the scene, A procession of top hats surmounting anxious faces would have been observable filing into one of the larger rooms at Paddington; seniors at the front, juniors at the back; the big gaffer and his entourage facing them from a high table.

A lengthy agenda would have been composed of suitable subjects for homilies and questions either from the great man himself or his experts; the audience of station masters. Although those present must have enjoyed it when that unpleasant lot at their neighbouring station were being held publically over a barrel, there was also the fear that the same could and would happen to themselves And, had there been closing times for licensed premises in the 1840s, at about a quarter to one there would no doubt have been a shortening of the homilies, and a drying up of the questions from the back of the room, to ensure that the agenda was finished in time for everyone to adjourn to more refreshing surroundings.

Such meetings have been going on ever since: whether the scene was Bristol, Birmingham, Wolverhampton or Worcester, (or Brighton, Bridlinton, Buxton or Berwick when referring to other 'lesser' companies), all held either in railway offices or a strategically placed hostelry, no doubt the pattern was much the same. Some meetings were for station masters only, some for goods agents only, and some for a mixture, in varied proportions, of the two.

The agenda was sent out some days before the meeting to give all those attending a chance to collect relevant statistics or to manufacture plausible excuses for any of the sins of their stations which they had a nasty feeling were going to be laid bare for all to see. Singly, or in groups that snow-balled in size as they got nearer to their destination, the victims made their way. Collars and hankies were clean, overcoats brushed, shoes blacked, smiles on faces not always very convincing. So, for the best part of a day, chief clerks and foremen successfully ran the railways: because, said the cynics, that was what they always did anyhow.

Station masters and goods agents who had the worst time of it were those from the medium sized stations. So little happened at the small ones, that their capacity for sin was strictly limited. One such station master who sat next to me had only to face one ball during the day's play. Asked why not a single passenger has joined an excursion train due to pick up at his station, he said that as even he had not been told that the train was running, it was not surprising that the public knew nothing about it either. Four neat runs!

For most much of their trouble was in keeping awake. They had been up early to check that all was well in their little kingdoms and they had got on thick woollen underwear more suitable for touring their coal sidings than for sitting in a centrally heated room where the temperature was about 70°.

One superintendent at Worcester aided their wakefulness by scanning the meeting at intervals, and, when he saw some bored individual beginning to nod off, would break off what he was saying to ask the offender if that was his experience at Defford, or wherever it was.

The large stations, passenger or goods, had the reputation of being so deep in turpitude that they were beyond praying for. Any criticisms of their suspect rostering of staff or bonus payments were better ventilated out of court where they would not put wrong ideas into other stations' heads. Furthermore, the gaffers of the large places were senior men whose guns matched those ranged against them from the top table. A non-aggression pact made good sense.

So it was the medium sized that had to take the strain. Waiting for their turn to come as each topic was discussed, some studied their statistics with knitted brows; others doodled or passed surreptitious notes to each other. One nervous gentleman at a meeting held in a hotel where the tables in the room had been prematurely laid for lunch, consumed three bread rolls during the course of the morning and had to make his peace with their rightful owners later on.

The top gaffers did not have it all their own way. At one meeting the young goods agent of a place that had been designated a New Town asked reasonably enough, why its station was to be closed. He said that in a few years time there would be a population of 60,000. "There will be no population of 60,000 in my lifetime," said the top gaffer, and added nastily "or in yours." "I am sorry, sir," replied the young man with a flashing Welsh smile, "that you give me such a poor expectation of life."

One of the oddest meetings I ever attended was soon after the war at Tipton Canal Baisin G.W. It was held out of doors on a hot day in the height of summer to demonstrate a new device that the makers claimed would take the place of capstans, shunt horses, and some shunting engines. The device looked like a cross between a car jack, a plough, and a motor cycle. It travelled on one wheel with flanges on either side to keep it on the rail; a jack-like shoe made contact with the underframe of the wagon it was to push; the motor bike engine supplied the power, while two plough-like handles stuck out behind for the operator to hold. An expert inspector had come from Paddington to show us what it could do.

Tipton Basin yard, never a very tidy place and then well on the way to extinction, was covered for much of the area with shoulder-high willow herb. Through this jungle, parting it in front of them as they walked, the meeting assembled. A truck of coal had been positioned at the end of one of the empty sidings with the device in position. The inspector explained to a suspicious audience how it worked and what it could do: then, after some difficulty and hard words,

the motor was started and off went the truck and the device up the siding followed by the meeting - like mourners at a funeral.

At the end of the siding was a turntable which the truck negotiated with difficulty, needing some helpful pushes from the meeting. The procession continued along the line past the stables where the two shunt horses, who had been given the day off, were watching events over the bottom door of their stable with intense interest. They were seen to exchange glances of surprise when they realised that their work was being done for them by this strange contraption. At this precise moment something went wrong; the device slipped from under the wagon and fell over with the engine racing and the wheel in the air where it was joined by the inspector's feet. The two horses burst into neighs of uninhibited laughter in which everyone except the inspector joined.

We were told to think it over and say if we could use one.

From 'Behind the Lines' by Christopher Burton.

FIRST, THIRD, OR HAMMOCK CLASS, SLEEPING CARS OF WW2

The oft quoted phrase, "Necessity is the mother of invention", has according to history been attributed to Plato, although scholars are at odds to definitely ascribe it to any one particular source. Whatever, the similar meaning term "Needs must" has been applied to industry and so far as this history is concerned, the railway system by numerous engineers, inventors and entrepreneurs from the age of Stephenson onwards. In recent times, meaning the past 40 or so years, the HST has been perhaps one of the best and long lived success stories, slightly further back in time, other ideas, Bulleid's 'Leader' class is what comes to mind here, were conceived out of a genuine belief that this was the way forward, and yet, was doomed to failure before the design had even left the drawing board let alone be turned into a solitary (badly) running prototype.

Be that as it may, it sometimes a brain such as that possessed by Bulleid that is needed to see beyond the obvious. To be able to reach what is nowadays deemed 'blue sky thinking' or to put another way, 'having eliminated the improbable what is left must be the most likely'.

In this way, we arrive then with a man (it must surely have been a man), who unknown by name, came up with a radical idea to suit a need at a time of want: or should that be "..to suit a want at a time of need"? Whatever, it was as radical, and to return to Bulleid again, as had been consider by the great man in the 1930s, for sleeping car bunks on the LNER to be wider at the top than at the toe. After all, as Bulleid had considered at the time, man is wider in the torso than at the feet, we might then save room by making a sleeping car bunk to the same design. Whilst fine in theory, it was not so in practice. The result resembled in shape a coffin. Indeed, according to Bulleid's first biographer, Sean Day-Lewis, the mock-up was so inscribed by an unknown at Doncaster. The lesson was learnt, but not before, it seems, the germ of an idea had been sown. It would bear fruit just a few years later.

That time would come during the dark days of WW2. The railways reaching capacity, passenger trains loaded to their maximum both so far as rolling stock and also passengers. It was, for example, almost impossible for a ticket collector to operate, and certainly impossible to find a seat let alone a spare berth in a sleeping car. Consequently with traffic from armed forces personnel reaching a peak, and many of these needing to travel on the longer distance routes from London to the north, a bright idea was formed relative to the sleeping cars then available. Why not, came the suggestion, replace the bunks: one per compartment in first-class and two per compartment in second-class, with hammocks? That way accommodation could be at least doubled, more so if wider hammocks for 'shared' use were considered for the top tier.

We know not who this idea emanated from, the obvious thought being a man with naval connections, or possible a member of staff from Doncaster who had in past been witness to the idea of Bulleid and his 'caskets'. Whatever, we can sure that if the scheme had been taken up fully, then a particular 'C.M.E.' would no doubt have claimed the credit, the fact it was subsequently not, means no one was prepared to acknowledge what was a unfortunate failure. But it so easily might not have been. After all were not sailors regularly sleeping in hammocks at sea and service personnel could similarly be found sleeping on luggage racks on trains?

Research at the National Archives, War Office papers, reveals concern expressed by the Admiralty, that sailors being recalled to their ship at short notice were arriving tired, having been forced to endure an often sleepless overnight journey - could it even be that the idea came from the Admiralty? There was real danger that at sea a man might not initially be alert enough in emergency. The result was a request to the Railway Executive for more sleeping car accommodation, but this was impossible at the time, hence the hammock principal.

Two existing sleeping car vehicles were selected, one from the east coast (LNER) and one from the west coast (LMS). The GWR were not involved although they did promise to monitor proceedings and act quickly if the trails proved successful.

In both cases the modified vehicles had the bunks stripped out and were replaced by, in first class, two hammocks one above the next, and a third suspended between the top of the door and window. Five were fitted in similar fashion to the second class although here the top-most was later changed to a double. The revised accommodation was advertised as available, the idea being for two to lie 'top and toe' in the large hammock. Luggage was evidently not considered and an obvious and initial problem quickly developed as servicemen invariably travelled with bulky kit-bags.

There were other disadvantages too. Passengers unused to hammock sleeping were similarly unprepared for the pitch and swing associated. It was not motion sickness that was the problem, more the risk of being tipped out on to the unfortunate individual in the hammock below at times of rough stops and starts.

Then there was the issue of the dual hammock. Some would attempt to avail themselves of 'home-comforts' -'Ladies of the Trains' as they quickly became known - the behaviour of which was hardly appreciated by the other occupants. Perhaps the worst recorded incident being when a rather portly Wren attempted to claim sole occupancy of the large hammock to the chagrin of the other individual with a genuine right to the same place. The result was, according to the subsequent witness statements, mayhem. A battle royal continued from Potters Bar almost to Perth, before said female was unceremoniously deposited, bottom first, on the face of a meek Midshipman below. The plaintiff cries prior to his unfortunate demise through shock were something none present ever wished to hear again.

It was incidents such as these, as well as those in a upper hammock, too drunk to care when nature called, that led to the rapid end of a theoretically good idea. In the end it was recognised that it would only be likely to work under levels of service discipline, not possible under railway operating conditions. Had the trial been successful then the files went on to say that much use could be made of parcels vehicles, segregated into accommodation for male and female travellers.

But in these days of ever increasing over-crowding on trains, might we may yet again one day consider such an idea for the delayed commuter?

DOG TICKETS

Speaking of dogs, as we have before, now may be the time to refer in more detail to this four-legged creature. Loved or loathed dependent upon one's viewpoint, they have been at the side of both railway staff and passengers probably since the earliest days.

As a pet, a dog affords comfort and companionship. The fact that for many years a licence was required for their existence, meant that in return the railway companies might charge for their conveyance. (The fee for an annual dog licence was for many years 7/6d [37.5p] but was abolished by parliament in 1987.)

The railway companies had different means of transporting dogs. 'Accompanied by a passenger' - perhaps that should really be 'passenger accompanied by a dog': as an item of livestock, consigned from one station to the next, and at times in a specially provided 'hound-van' which as the name implies, were used when a pack of hounds might be transported over a distance invariably in connection with the hunt.

Some companies, notably the Southern Railway and Great Western (so presumably the others as well) would issue a set-price ticket allowing travel for one dog to a station within a specific radius of the departure point. This then obviated the need for separate dog tickets to be provided to countless destinations. Perhaps it is surprising this seemingly simple method of accountancy was not similarly applied to humans also.

Whatever, the system worked well for many years, that is until on one occasion the ticket collector demanded tickets from her lady passenger and seven - it might have been more - accompanying dogs. The protestations that it had been one passenger and one dog when they boarded the train, but delays en-route allied to the rough riding had caused the dog to give birth, were not considered acceptable. We are not told if the excess charge was in the end successfully applied to the new puppies.

But dogs have not just been involved with railways on the basis of accruing revenue. They have been employed by the railway in varying roles from early days - receptacles for collecting money for railway charity, certainly in the latter case a number of different animals were used, each with a saddle-type collecting tin attached to its back and which animal would then be led across the station concourse and sometimes even through the actual train.

When the poor creature reached the end of its life a number were 'stuffed and mounted' so as to continue collecting but now based on sympathy. Many readers, of middle-aged and beyond, will no doubt recall seeing the results of such taxidermy on display in glass cases at various important stations. Like so many other memories of the past, they were there one day and then disappeared, somehow no longer in keeping with modern society. Fortunately one of these 'former' collecting dogs has been 're-homed' and continues to perform its original purpose on a preserved railway. (We are told the taxidermy was also overhauled…).

Then there were other uses for dogs - and other animals as well. Horses were used for shunting and cartage work, cats were regularly on the payroll as the catchers of vermin, whilst felines might also be a resident in a particular shed, signal box or station - that is if a cat is ever 'resident' anywhere - independent creatures as they are. Under such circumstances the men themselves: often burly,

perhaps on occasions even outspoken and opinionated, but woo-betide anyone who ever dared mistreat the resident cat. It would not be the feline who would be in need of nine lives under such situations.

To return to specifics and this time the story of a particular sheepdog by the name of Sammy. Renowned for his herding skills, Sammy was thus much in demand 'at stud'. It was on one his ventures to father the next generation that story commences.

Sammy had travelled before and similarly been successfully retuned. This in the period when rail travel was the preferred choice to the charabanc, and a 'motor' was not available to the likes of Sammy's owner.

A strong wicker basket, the necessary label, 'Name, destination, route, and most importantly - instructions on water stops' was affixed to the basket and probably with a final lick to his master he settled down comfortably for another journey.

The distance was perhaps 100 miles, part of the route one which, if he had known, he had been over before, but the final distance and destination would be new and as such, involve a change of train as well as travel over a different company's line.

All went well to start. Two hours later at the junction a porter, alerted by the guard, opened Sammy's basket and he was let out for a drink - and no doubt to inspect the nearest platform lamp. (To him I suppose it was, 'Any post in a storm'), but then something happened which could not have been foreseen. On the opposite side of the platform was the station goods yard, and at one end was a pen where coincidentally some sheep were being loaded. One of these woolly creatures - possibly slightly overweight due to having been on the 'fresh grass diet', managed to force its way from the pen through wooden fencing that had long seen better days and was last seen aiming towards the end of the yard closely followed by several of its colleagues. No amount of shouting or gesturing from startled porters or local farmers had any effect, if anything it worsened the situation. The signalman meanwhile, in his cabin at the end of the yard was now faced with a dilemma, what was the bell-code to the next box for 'sheep running away on right

line', and 'wrong line' for that matter, as the woolly brained creatures seemed determined to cross and re-cross from up to down and back to up again. Sammy had observed this, initially with quiet distain We cannot imagine what his doggy brain must have been considering, but obviously a connection was made at some stage for he was next seen dashing off at top speed having wrenched the holding piece of string from the hand of the porter to which he had been attached and was clearly in hot pursuit. Another signalling dilemma, what was the code for 'two (or more) animals in the same section' (and not coupled together). None was displaying a tail lamp either, somehow a flapping piece of string and paper label did not count.

Anyway, the sheep evidently got fed up with wandering along the ballast and made their way into a nearby field - sheep will find an opening anywhere given the chance - whilst Sammy eventually lost interest and made his way onward. Dogs can also be resourceful and so eventually just like the well know Lassie story he found his way home, it was no the full 100 miles of course, in fact probably no more than about 15 across country, to arrive back in his familiar farmyard much to the relief of owner, railway and the like. I am told consigning farmer demanded, and received, a full refund, whether Sammy was ever send away again is not reported. And I promise not to recount further his exploits for fear of turning these pages into a proper 'shaggy dog story'.

Purfectly true - did you know the station master at Chipping Norton kept a pet pig for many years.

Its photo even appearing in the GWR staff magazine. Pigs are in fact highly intelligent and do indeed make excellent pets. So having quoted the 100% truth now for the fantasy (but which could equally be true). Presumably it had a name - 'banger' perhaps?

WHITER THAN WHITE Part 2

(or should it be 'What a way to run a railway?')

by Alan Cooksey, former Chief Inspecting Officer - Railways

In order to build a new railway Parliamentary approval was – and still is – required, but during the boom in railway building that occurred in the late 1830s, concerns grew that new railways were being opened to traffic before they were finished, resulting in some terrible accidents. In 1840 'An Act for Regulating Railways' was passed. Included in its provisions was a requirement that new railways should be inspected before they opened to traffic.

In 1840 Government regulation of how companies went about their business was rare and the reasons behind the creation of powers to inspect the new railways had more to do with ensuring that investment in railways would continue and less about concerns for those being killed and injured.

Initially, an Inspector-General was appointed to examine and report on the projects submitted to the Board of Trade and carefully examine all new lines after construction. In 1840 the construction of the new railways was largely in the hands of engineers who were members of the Institution of Civil Engineers and the only alternative source of engineering expertise available – and therefore independent to those building the railways – were military engineers.

Thus the first Inspecting Officers of Railways were serving military officers seconded to the Railway Inspectorate and subsequently retired officers from the Royal Engineers, many with a wide experience of operating military railways, were appointed. The tradition of Inspecting Officers being army officers continued until the first non-army engineer became an Inspecting Officer some 140 years after the creation of the Inspectorate.

The 1840 Act had one basic flaw. Railways that were inspected and found unfit to open opened anyway. The 1840 Act had powers to inspect but not to prevent the

railway opening. This loophole was closed by the Regulation of Railways Act 1842 ('An Act for the better Regulation of Railways and for the Conveyance of Troops').

The 1842 Act also included requirements for the railway companies to report accidents and from the beginning Inspecting Officers investigated railway accidents.

However, it was not until 1871 when 'An Act to amend the Law respecting the Inspection and Regulation of Railways' was passed that the powers to investigate accidents were set out. The Railway Inspectorate basically undertaking its original functions and with only relatively minor updates to the legislation used for 160 years. The Railway Inspectorate only became HM Railway Inspectorate in its later years. Today it no longer exists; its role having been split between the Office of Rail Regulation and the Rail Accident Investigation Branch.

The role of an Inspecting Officer not only required them to be determinedly independent but also to have the strength to deal with situations that, frequently in undertaking accident investigations were both very serious and unpleasant. It is not surprising therefore that many below the surface had an almost outrageous sense of humour and on occasions could get up to some exploits that must have taken aback the contractor's engineers and senior railway officers involved.

TUNNEL VISION

F.R. Conder in his book 'The men who built the railways' * first published in 1868, has a chapter on the activities of Inspecting Officers and not always in the most flattering of terms. Among the stories of is one of General Paisley inspecting a tunnel that was lined with masonry for a short distance from either portal. General Paisley decided that the most appropriate way of testing the unlined portion of the tunnel was to fire wooden projectiles at the roof of the tunnel and a small party of sappers led by a corporal from the Royal Engineers complete with mortar and necessary ammunition duly arrived and fire several projectiles at the tunnel roof. We are not informed of the consequences.* Reprinted by Thomas Telford Ltd in 1983

BEST FOOT FORWARD

Notwithstanding that as the number of new railways being built diminished, the number of changes being made to existing railways all of which required approval by the Inspectorate increased. Among the things that had to be submitted were changes to track layouts and signalling.

A process that applied for much of the lifetime of the Inspectorate was for a 'provisional approval' to be given following a study of the documents and then for an Inspecting Officer to carry out an inspection when the works were completed. It was probably open to debate as to whether the granting of provision approval had any legal basis but it was an effective way of working. As a senior Government lawyer said on one occasion, when the legal powers of the Inspectorate were being discussed, "...whether the Inspecting Officers have the legal powers to do something has never worried them in the past".

It was the role of the Inspecting Officer to make sure what was being inspected was safe, thus doing something that was unlikely and had not been foreseen occasionally found things that had been overlooked by the railway operators and engineer. Indeed what an Inspecting Officer was going to examine and test when the inspection was made was not always as unstructured as at first it might have appeared. Thus the study of submitted documents may well have identified something that should be examined during the inspection. However, on some occasions it was more a case of intuition during the inspection rather that identified something that was not right. Inspecting Officers undertaking inspections had the freedom to indulge in all sorts of activities, which, if a railway employee had copied similar would have got them in serious trouble with the railway management.

The mechanical interlocking that lies behind – or more frequently below – a signal box lever frame is designed to prevent the signalmen pulling a combination of levers that would set up a conflicting route and possibly lead to derailment or a collision between trains. Sometimes when alterations were made to the track layout and signalling the resulting changes to the mechanical interlocking could be difficult to make and alternative ideas and solutions were considered by the signal engineers.

One story told within the Inspectorate was about Col. John Robertson a former Chief Inspecting Officer when inspecting a mechanical signal box. He asked the railway officers why two of the levers, close together in the lever frame had been fitted with foot treadles. He was informed that the treadles had been fitted so that the signalman had to stand with his foot on the treadle to pull either of the levers and was thus prevented from pulling the other lever at the same time. When asked if the interlocking would allow this the railway officers confirmed it would but by installing the treadles on the levers any risk that a conflicting route could be set up by the signalman had been removed

It is said that Col. Robertson having listened to the explanation took hold of both levers and attempted to pull them together. Of course, nothing happened. He then first stood on one treadle and then placed his other foot on the other treadle and still holding onto the two levers launched himself backward simultaneously pulling both levers. Telling an Inspecting Officer that something could not be done was always likely to be regarded as a challenge to try.

HEAD-ON

Damage to line-side fencing has always been a problem for the railway and so while conducting an inspection Lt. Col. Townsend-Rose saw a length of new fence that had been particularly badly vandalised. Without hesitation he climbed through the damaged fence, crossed the road and banged on the front door of one of the houses that bordered the railway. The door opened only for the Colonel to be confronted by a rather angry and very large and muscular man in a none to clean vest. With the Railway Officers fearing that Col. Townsend-Rose was about to be physically assaulted, Col. Townsend-Rose undeterred proceeded to firmly tell the man about his responsibility to stop vandalism to the fencing.

IMAGINATION REQUIRED

High voltage overhead electrification of the railway created differing safety issues and Inspecting officers would make a site inspection before the catenary was energised. The risk of metal theft required inspections as quickly as possible after it was erected. Mr Alan Cooksey, the first non-military Inspecting Officer, arrived at Wolverhampton where an extension of the existing electrification was being undertaken to find that although the line-side masts had been erected there was no overhead catenary in place. When Mr Cooksey suggested that might make his inspection a little difficult, it was suggested with his knowledge of such systems he could he not use his imagination as to what it would look like. Approval was not given.

STUCK

Some years later as part of his investigation of the collision at Colwich Junction Maj. Olver ran another test train. The train was driven towards the junction at the speeds the evidence suggested and brake applications made at the appropriate places. The test was carried out with all the lines closed to traffic and with the junction set for the branch to Stoke. The test train travelled through the junction and stopped beyond it. Satisfied that much of the evidence had been confirmed, it was agreed that the train that was across the junction and completely blocking the West Coast main line should now be moved as quickly as possible. Unfortunately it would not move. The locomotive had come to a stand perfectly centred beneath the short permanently electrically isolated neutral section in the overhead catenary.

A CHANGE OF CLOTHES

As well as operating within the United Kingdom, the Inspectorate from time to time carried out a similar role for the Governments of Hong Kong and Singapore. Maj. Peter Olver undertaking inspections of new Metro stations in Singapore asked about the arrangements for manually inching an escalator to release someone whose clothing or

perhaps a foot had got trapped. He was assured that the station staff had been trained in how to do it. A metal flap had to be lifted in the platform and this gave access to a hand wheel. The person turning the wheel had to sit on the platform with their feet in the open pit astride the wheel. Maj. Olver removed one of his shoes and pushed his sock under the 'comb plate' at the end of the escalator. The member of staff on the platform was a lady and having said that she knew what to do, disappeared for several minutes. She then returned having changed from her uniform skirt into a pair of trousers to allow her to sit astride the wheel.

THE STATION CAT

The Inspectorate was extensively involved in providing advice during the construction of the Hong Kong Mass Transit Railway and Inspecting Officers carried out inspections of the new lines as the system was expanded. Major Tony King and Mr Alan Cooksey were charged with the inspection of the Island Line immediately prior to its approval to be opened to passenger service. The normal inspection procedure was if the Inspecting Officer identified something that might be a safety issue it was discussed with the railway managers who accompanied him and agreement reached on what was needed to be done. One of the party being responsible for recording the notes of the inspection.

During Maj. King's inspection of one the stations, he notice that a cat was following the inspection party. The Inspecting Officer said that the cat should be feed fresh fish twice a week. Obviously, this was not the sort of issued raised by an Inspecting Officer and included as a condition to the recommendation that the railway was safe to open but the manager taking notes wrote it down and it was included in the formal notes of the inspection.

Years later Mr Cooksey while undertaking another inspection visited the station and curled up in a corner of the control room was a cat. There had been several cats since the one that had accompanied Maj. King on the first inspection, but the Station Manager eagerly explained that the cat was still feed fresh fish twice a week as required by the Inspectorate.

WHAT EVERY LAYOUT NEEDS!

Multi-Scale

AVAILABLE AT ALL GOOD MODEL SHOPS

See reverse of packet for instructions for use

Instructions for use – Shake over the layout where required until sufficient
gremlins are dispersed to create the desired effect.

HEALTH WARNING – ONLY TO BE USED BY EXPERIENCED MODELLERS WITH A SENSE OF HUMOUR

CHARLES DICKENS? - IT MOST CERTAINLY IS NOT

Many readers will recall the excellent BBC one-off programme of some years ago, 'The Signalman' based on the short story by Dickens. No doubt there have been several adaptations, the BBC variant (available on DVD at one time) was filmed on the Severn Valley Railway using, I am told, interior shots of Arley signal box plus a purpose built exterior near one end of Foley tunnel. Strict accuracy in railway operation was not given, but I for one did not bother with such trivia, the atmosphere nonetheless was perfectly created resulting in a programme I could, and indeed have, watched time and time again.

Railways and indeed ships lend themselves wonderfully to the imagination of the writer. Indeed countless books and short-stories have been penned over the years using such themes as horror, the occult, crime, romance, comedy, children's stories etc. Who can forget 'Close Encounters', 'The Signalman' - already mentioned, 'The First Great Train Robbery', 'Thomas the Tank Engine', and my own personal favourite 'Ivor the Engine' (well actually it was the 'Great St Trinians Train Robbery' that was favourite, but at my age the thought of all those supposed sixth-formers cavorting around is probably too much for the body to cope with). Instead let us turn to fiction based on fact, not a ghost story as such, but one which certainly has an unexpected ending and which, dependent upon the perception of the reader, may be seen as the imagination or even a mistake by the principal player, or even something much more mysterious.

Having, I hope, enticed the reader to continue, let me start. The locations are exactly accurate, the period also, the names of the players altered only in as much as I promised not to reveal these. One male, who we shall call Philip, and one female, the name of which was never revealed although the initial was 'J'.

Picture the scene, a grimy Paddington station in 1946. The clock is just after 5.00 pm and in consequence of the rush hour there are countless, passengers, porters, parcels, barrows and the like all forming part of the early evening scene. (I have always thought that when one finishes work at the end of the day it should be evening not afternoon.) Amongst the crowd is a tall man walking slowly towards the train on Platform 3. He walks alone but carries a small leather brief case. He is dressed in a rain-coat of the period, and hat. Nothing unremarkable, indeed he is exactly as per the fashion of the time, blending in with the masses. No one you would notice in a crowd. He walks towards the country end of Platform 3 and there opens the door to an empty compartment in a non-corridor clerestory coach. The sort of vehicle that should really have been pensioned off from main line service years before, but had been retained, albeit not for much longer, due to the necessities of war. The choice of carriage was deliberate, with no corridor access he would not be disturbed once the train was moving. Having seated himself, with 'back to the engine', the briefcase was placed on the bench seat alongside, the coat and hat removed and placed nearby.

As seen this was the face of a sad man, someone who had endured tragedy and yet had not yet, privately at least, come to terms with the circumstances. Publically there was the persona of a stable individual, but away from the crowd he was withdrawn, still unable to accept that an enemy bomb had destroyed his life, taking away family and home, the very things he held most dear. With no home in London remaining and certainly no wish to be continually reminded within the City, he had sought a complete change, a village called Sutton Scotney in Hampshire, accessible by train through Newbury, albeit a lengthy and time consuming journey exacerbated by the restricted service south of Newbury. Consequently he worked a six day week, his employer happy to allow a shorter working day spread over six days - it also meant his mind was more occupied - less time to dwell on the sound, the sight, which had been there less than two years earlier.

The general disadvantage of a non-corridor clerestory was no access to the restaurant car on what was a Weymouth bound service, although in some respects that was probably best. Such places were limited in the offerings available whilst the number of forces personnel travelling meant it was far from the quiet sanctuary he sought. Consequently his case contained a Thermos and it was this he was accessing just as the train started to move.

Every day up to now he had also relaxed at this point, the first indication of movement a time for him to start the unwinding process. He would be unlikely to be joined now, no corridor meant no access, whilst the stop at Reading usually saw more passengers leaving rather than joining. But today would be different. Today something would happen that would change his life and leave him wondering for the rest of his days. And it started just as he reached across to grasp his flask.

At that point he was no longer looking at the platform, the initial fore and aft motion of the train all he was aware of. But then trains started slowly compared with today, and he was suddenly disturbed from his inner thoughts by the carriage door opening and a female passenger stumbling in. The door clanged behind and there was the fleeting glimpse of a porter nearby - no need to lower the droplight and turn the handle at least. Then as the train began to accelerate past the end of the platform Philip was conscious also of someone running alongside the ballast trying it seemed to grasp the carriage and haul himself aboard. It all happened in an instant, one minute there was this figure running, then he was gone, tripped probably, hopefully not under the wheels. 'The guard would have noticed' he thought, and with that any idea of pulling the communication cord was banished. Besides, the train was still accelerating so clearly nothing must have happened.

Philip turned his gaze to within the compartment and whilst trying not to stare he looked at the woman opposite. Smartly dressed but obviously nervous, he assumed distressed in some form, whilst she held a hankerchief to her mouth and stared out of the window. 'Did you see that man?' he found himself asking, 'The one who was trying to jump on the train'. She turned to look at his, 'Yes…', there was pause, 'Did he get on she asked?', the question was phrased almost with desperation. Philip recognised the signs and tried to be controlled, 'No, he stumbled, but I think he was alright'. The response was received with a look he could not quite make out. Relief, concern, fear - it could been any of these, but equally none.

They continued in silence. The idea of a drink from his flask totally forgotten. But as the train passed through the western suburbs, so easily identified with the smells associated with the various factories, curiosity got the better of him. After all she was undoubtedly an attractive lady, well dressed and from the few words she had uttered so far, well educated, he noticed too there were no rings, what other jewellery she had was tastefully worn.

He decided the best course was an offer, 'Would you like some tea, it may be a bit stewed by now but it is the only option as there is no corridor to the restaurant car?' He realised at once it was a poor statement and one that was also blindingly obvious. For a moment he wished he had said nothing but she turned from gazing out of the window and in a soft voice spoke, her voice now calm and in control. 'No thank you, but it was very kind of you to ask. I am so sorry if I disturbed you, you clearly chose this carriage as you wished to be alone.' It was a quick and considered response. One which meant she had summed up the situation and yet also allowed him the opportunity of taking the conversation further should he wish, or to smile slightly in acknowledgement and then he to could continue to gaze out through the window.

He chose the former, starting with, 'You seemed to be in a hurry, you are alright I hope…..if I can help at all…?' It was said more as a statement rather than a question, but this time she smiled, replying, 'It is very kind of you, I am alright really, I was just trying to get on the train, without for once being followed.' Again it was a response that could be ignored or taken further. She was still looking across the carriage at him and so once again he attempted speech. This time it was easier, he found himself explaining, in part at least his own life, in the hope she too might open up to him. The more he looked the more he found her attractive. Hair short, little make up, and as she responded, a calm and sympathetic approach. It had been a long time since he had spoken this way to any woman Since the death of Sally he had shunned female contact, too afraid that something might one day happen again to destroy his life. He began to wish the train journey would last forever, although some days it did indeed seem to, arrears of maintenance meant bottlenecks and diversions were commonplace, a two hour journey on occasions taking twice the time and meaning that more than once he had been stranded in Newbury having missed the last train south.

As they spoke he learned about her. How with parents in Scotland she had come to London to work, her fiancée killed in action and how she worked in a government office in London. She had an Aunt in Newbury and was making her way there in the hope of escaping a man who had been following her for some time. It was not an attempted relationship but one where there appeared to be a more sinister intent. She did not say if it was this man who had tripped and stumbled alongside and he did not like to ask.

Suddenly though as if she had said enough she stopped, touched his knee gently and said, 'Thank you, I have probably bored you and said far too much.' Again it was a signal that could have been taken either way, and he, not wishing to push further sat back on his own side, she likewise, both now staring, probably at the same nothingness, out of the side window.

With a jerk the brakes came on after which a clatter of pointwork under the carriage indicated the arrival at Reading. As at Paddington the platform was crowded, but here those stood might have been waiting for trains heading for any number of different destinations and consequently when they left a few minutes later they were still alone. All the time they were stationery she looked nervous. Peering back along the platform as well as to the doors almost as if half expecting someone to deliberately enter the carriage from either side and join them.

Phillip knew their journey would end in less than half an hour and spoke again, 'Look I know we are both getting out at Newbury, but if there is anything I can do, escort you to your aunt, whatever, please let me know'. She smiled again, 'You are very kind, but you have another train to catch, and if you do come with me you will miss it, you have already told me there are no others this evening.' He was annoyed with himself. For whatever reason he was desperately attracted to this woman. One who smiled gently, not appearing to judge and yet one who eyes it seemed could peer within him almost to the very depths of his soul. He spoke again, 'I meant it, I would like to help if I can'.

She spoke, 'Let me talk to my Aunt first. I will probably be on the same train tomorrow evening, perhaps we might speak further then.' It was an invitation and one which now made him wish it was tomorrow already.

The train rumbled on, past sleepy villages and stations. Theale, Aldermaston, Midgham and Thatcham before again the brakes were applied on the approach to Newbury. Phillip stood up to open the door, as he did he noticed it had started to drizzle, the droplets highlighted against the gas lamps on the platform which hissed and spitted in their usual fashion. She thanked him and took his hand when it was offered to help in alighting. Again he noticed the quick glance, almost as if there was concern as to who might be present, but she relaxed again. The few passengers were already making their way to the exit or walking, as he would soon, towards the bay platform where the Southampton train waited.

Her hand lingered perhaps slightly longer than it should. She spoke, 'Thank you. Thank you for being so kind. I really would like to speak to you again, perhaps…..' Her words tailed off. He spoke, 'Tomorrow will be fine, I look forward to it'. He turned to close the carriage door conscious the train would be waiting to leave, and as he did so he noticed a hankerchief where she had been sat. Reaching inside he took it, in so doing letting go of her hand. When he emerged a moment later she was already walking down the platform. The thought was to run after her but his own train was waiting and due to depart immediately after the Weymouth service. If he missed it he would be stranded in Newbury. He watched her walk until she turned through the exit without a backward glance. Certain there would be the opportunity the next day he put in his pocket and made his way to his own train.

The journey south from Newbury was accomplished without incident. The guard opening the door of his compartment to ask for his ticket, but this was a regular occurrence, as was the extinguishing of the platform lamps as they left the various Hampshire stations. Sutton Scotney was reached on time. Phillip made his way across the board crossing and out across the forecourt. From here he walked down the slope to the main road before turning right the few hundred yards to his cottage. Home was a small 'two up - two down' end of terrace. Plain and simple, a photograph on the dresser displaying a couple in happier times.

A meal was ate in silence followed by an attempt at some paperwork he had brought home, then a bath and a restless night. Work followed the next day, his regular routine. He did scour the platform at Newbury that morning, likewise the crowds leaving his train at Paddington. There was just a chance, but she was not there.

That evening he arrived in plenty of time. The same type of stock was in use and he hesitated whether to wait at the barrier or on the platform. As departure time came he took his seat as per the day before, alone once more and now becoming ever more anxious. She did not arrive and again there was no sign at Newbury. In fact for the remainder of his commuting days he was never to see her again. A chance meeting, a handkerchief which he had kept, embroidered with the initial 'J' and a memory, all that remained and with them so many unanswered questions.

Years later Philip would retire, still living in the same cottage at Sutton Scotney, whilst later still the railway line through the village was closed and no longer would he be disturbed at night by the occasion train. His story was told to me years later. A mystery never solved, a mystery combining both intrigue and affection, one so real for so short a time but then, like time itself, a transitory occurrence destined never to be repeated. Philip is no more, he never remarried. Those who knew him recalled that in his later years he would often be seen staring, wondering, a man for whom life had created a question he was never able to answer.

Newbury - Winchester (Sutton Scotney) train in the bay.

NIGHT SHIFT - PART 1

All Saints Church was just across the road from Hockley Depot in Birmingham. It has been pulled down now, but in the 1950s its bells used to play hymn tunes in the evenings. A particularly favourite hymn was, 'Now the day is over' which included the lines:-

Birds and beasts and flowers soon will be asleep.

The shunters in the North End cabin, thus serenaded as they arrived for the night shift, felt that the vicar could have been a bit more sensitive in his choice of theme. He, doubtless, like the birds and the beasts, would soon have his head down: but not them. They were on until six in the morning. Yet, once you had accepted it as a fact of life, the night shift had its good points. Partly, perhaps, because the other two turns also had their drawbacks. The early turn meant getting out of bed at 4.15 a.m. and, in winter, an excruciatingly foul journey through dark, wet or frosty, and sometimes snow covered streets to get to work by six o'clock. The late turn, though it had advantages for gardeners with a morning at home, was anti-social. You were cut off from all social life as completely as if you had been an inmate of that establishment just down the line at Winson Green.

In some ways the night shift had a touch of romance. Out in the yard for the first part of the turn, the outwards freight services ran into the loop at intervals, their great engines dwarfing our pannier tanks. One after another they departed: the 'London', the 'Bristol', the 'Westbury', the 'Birkenhead', and the Ponty'. After that for a spell all was quiet. Close to the cabins, the shunting engines dozed, softly hissing to themselves. The bobbing lights of handlamps vanished from the yard; the smell of bacon replaced the smell of steam. Then the tide began to flow in. Arthur, the yard inspector, high up in his sanctum next to the South End shunters' cabin, could feel an in-coming train in his bones long before it came into the loop. He trimmed the wick of his lamp and buttoned up the collar of his overcoat; then, looking round the door of the cabin, gave his head a backward jerk which all inside understood. Five minutes later, his head repeated this jerk at the North End cabin. The bobbing lights of handlamps re-appeared; the shunting engines shook

themselves and rolled off to work; first a trip from Bordesley, then the 'Bristol', the 'London', and so on.

On the goods shed the atmosphere on nights was happy and informal. Many of the staff had already been on overtime from six until nine which left them an hour to fill in before they started work again. Those who devoted this hour to a cup of cocoa and reading an improving book were few and far between: three rival attractions across the road were available according to their choice of brewer. The only time in the year when this practice went too far was on 'Paddy's Day', March 17., when the Irish contingent were liable to march in through the time office singing "When Irish eyes are smiling" to the accompaniment of a squeeze-box.

Experienced supervisors were well aware of the unwisdom of up-setting Irishmen at turning-out time - on 'Paddy's Day' of all days, even when they were supposed to be starting work. The sing-song continued in the mess room until snores superseded the 'Rose of Tralee'. Quietly, we booked them off from the start of the shift: and, being the fair-minded men that most of them were, they never complained.

Most of the work for the night shift on the shed consisted of un-loading wagons that had arrived during the day or came in during the night. But sometimes fate, in the shape of a temporary fall-off in traffic or an excess of zeal by the other two shifts in unloading more than their share, left the night gangs with little work to do. This was the signal for 'cut-sweeping'.

There were nine platform roads in Hockley's two-hundred-wagon shed, most of them grouped in pairs with a platform on either side. The space occupied by the double track between the platforms was the 'cut'. Before the loaders started to fill their allotted wagons, they were supposed to sweep them out. In theory, the resulting rubbish should have been placed on a trolley and taken round to the truck thoughtfully provided for the purpose on No. 9 Road. A quicker method was to stuff it all down between the wagons and the platform: and this they did.

From 'Behind the Lines' by Christopher Burton.

Sooner rather than later, the condition of the cut got so foul that not only was there a danger of derailments but also of peculiar smells - Even Felix, the station cat, gave a wide berth to a place where a broken cask of sausage skins had joined the straw, brick-ends, fish meal and old sacking.

We chose the gangs for cut-sweeping by getting their checkers to draw lots from the foreman's hat. Those who got landed for the job were exempt next time round. I always thought it unfair that the loaders were exempt from this dirty job, as, under the 'Sam-and-the-musket' principle, they should have been the first to qualify. The roads selected for sweeping were kept clear of wagons except for strategically placed ovens to remove the rubbish. Dolefully, half of the party worked along the lines, throwing the stuff up on to the platform. The other half followed along behind shovelling the heaps into their open wagon which they pushed along with them. Then, as soon as they had finished, they could go home.

In the 1950s people were not so security minded as they are now; doors and gates were left open at night which today would be locked. As a result, in those days we used to get a regular crop of uninvited guests at night from among those who slept rough. There were probably far more of them than we ever discovered, but two came to life in most un-usual places. One had installed himself in a large cupboard close to the radiator in the room used by the crane-drivers; reverberating snores gave him away. The other, who had a preference for more fresh air, had made up a bed for himself, with straw pads and a cartage sheet, between the lines where they passed under a bascule bridge on the shed. Lifting the bridge, the shunters prodded the sleeper with their pole; they pointed out that the engine was about to pass over and suggested that he tried somewhere else. He took their advice.

The trouble was not confined to visitors from outside. One night, the foreman and I were searching for one Tom, a checker who we knew had started work but disappeared. We looked everywhere without success. Now there was on shed a loaded who belonged to that group of humanity who, through they do little themselves, make a study of knowing what other people are doing and even thinking.

'Looking for Tom?' asjked this loader as the foreman and I went past. We said we were. 'Try the Glasgow', said the loader.

We had already looked in the 'Glasgow' once; it was nearly empty, a large box in one corner and a pile of straw in the other. On this second visit, the foreman kicked the pile of straw and encountered something soft. We had found Tom: he rose like a sleepy Venus from waves of straw, blinking in the light of the handlamp.

NIGHT SHIFT - PART 2

I have never been a true railwayman, well I was once for three months part-time, whilst I also did a few days as a freelance for the WR Public Affairs Department and had a consultancy role for a few years helping to sift records at Porchester Road, but I hardy think any of this qualifies me to wear the office of a professional. But I have done shift work, for many years in fact, and I can relate exactly the effect such varying start times can have on the digestion as well as the social life. (Personally I found trying to sleep on a hot summers morning was the worst - windows open in an attempt to capture any possible breeze but at the same time allowing in the sounds of DIY, people and everyday noise.)

However I digress.

My own shift work started back in the early 1970s when as a young 'Dixon of Dock Green' I spent some months wandering the streets of Southampton at night - it was always nights, never day turns - to 'show a presence' at what was the time of a spate of local arson attacks.

Having had I will admit a fairly sheltered upbringing, police work had been an eye-opened, not least when I was allotted the then 'Red-Light area' of Southampton to walk around. Forty plus years ago this was a time when the 'goods available' were openly displayed inside the windows of various terrace houses - I say displayed - well the packaged goods were at least. The same product accompanied by illuminated neon signs, 'New Model'. 'Latest Model' and the like. (Someone has since told me there was one which said 'Reconditioned Model', but I personally cannot recall.)

I suspect the sergeant deliberately allotted me this 'beat' due to my naivety, 'sink or swim' his likely motto. I will freely admit to being terrified, of course nothing did happen although several times movement was seen scurrying away down dark alleyways, whilst curtains would twitch and what flesh that had been exposed was rapidly covered up as I walked past.

I recall wandering aimlessly down Hartington Road at Northam, where on the other side of a concrete wall was Northam Junction signal box. Here I would stand listening to bells ringing and levers crashing at the same time wondering also if my choice of career had in fact been correct. Clearly I was visible to the signalman on duty, who seeing me illuminated by a nearby streetlight was quick to made drinking motions with his hand. Police training school might have taught me some things, the recognised sign for tea not appearing in Moriarty's Police Law, but it was still known of all the same.

I quickly discovered that if an innocent looking nail was pulled out of the concrete wall, it was possible to stand on this, like the rung of a ladder, and so reach over to unlock the inset door that led on to railway property. Care being taken to push the nail back again to avoid unwanted visitors. Within a few minutes I had established my credentials and a few minutes later was working the box - under supervision of course.

For every night afterwards I would specially request the same 'beat', so much so that some of my colleagues began to suspect I may have found some particular means of entertainment. One of two of my colleagues also appeared to ask rather pointed questions, I suspect they were concerned I might have been trespassing on their own ground! I gave nothing away, leaving them to draw their own conclusions.

It could not last. My downfall was not the lady at No 15, or even her at No 73, instead it was the simple matter of a police radio. Every time I visited the signal box I naturally turned the volume down, it was important that if a phone rang in the box, as it often did, there was no risk of a radio squeaking into life especially if were 'control' on the line.

Unfortunately one night my own control room had been trying to call me and with the volume down low I simply did not hear. When I failed to respond it appears they sent out a posse in the mistaken belief I had been injured or worse still, taken prisoner inside No 44!

After that it was the High Street and Above Bar, not quite the same. And I never did get to try No 73.

'Incident at Madder Bridge, Whimshire'

'Feelings run high when a wayward railway wagon smashes through the parapet of the bridge over the Myrtle Canal; at Rose Madder and Hookers Green halt (the thatched shelter on the right)). A half-timbered signal box here controls the crossing of the PBLR main line by an industrial railway conveying barrels to and from the Madder Carmine Company works. These are transported by canal narrow-boat, having gained access to the lower level via somewhat hazardous looking lift. The PBLR would of course much prefer to carry all this traffic but the MVVo., having its own boats based at nearby Hookers Green Wharf, is proudly independent. Local predictions that the Madder Lake is about to run dry have proved false and trade remains buoyant.'

©Peter Barnfield

WATER, GAS and ELECTRICITY

The Great Western was always, in theory at least, very economy conscious. For instance, in an old G. W. booklet that came to light when we were clearing out a cupboard at Kidderminster, there was an instruction to stationmasters, goods agents, and other persons in charge to ensure that the bars of soap issued to them from Swindon were to be cut into cakes and dried in the sun before use. This was to make them last longer.

The same booklet laid it down that all pins should be salvaged from super-annuated correspondence and, if they were not rusty, used again. It would have been disloyal to have called the company mean: but they certainly were careful.

So it was not surprising that when it came to the consumption of water, gas, and electricity, headquarters made quite certain that stations and depots, both great and small, sent in regular returns showing how much they had used. The printed forms provided had spaces for the figures for this year; the figures for the same period last year; and a generous space in which to explain any variation, up or down.

Apart from the explanations, water presented few problems; except for those who had to read the meters. These were hidden away in the most unlikely and inaccessible places. The bodily contortions required to read the figures cost many a portly foreman the back buttons on his trousers. Wiser foremen gave the job to their lad-porters who were more lissome.

Explanations were not easy. Particularly so where there were figures for two sorts of water, drinking and otherwise, which could, and did get mixed up. It was no use putting a comfortably vague remark such as "more locos using column this year", against the drinking water figures: District office would reply with a sarcastic memo by return.

Old hands at the correspondence game tried to lure the district office away into corresponding with other departments and other stations. Thus, a comment such as "shunting engine requiring more water on arrival this year" implied that it was the footplatemen who had changed the place of refreshment of their engine and, therefore, no fault

From 'Behind the Lines' by Christopher Burton.

of yours. If the critical clerk at district office was fool enough to try to follow up a lead like that, his efforts would soon peter out in a sand-drag of unanswered memos. Otherwise reliance had to be placed on explanations such as "burst pipe last year" to explain a decrease; or "fire practice this year" for an increase.

At Netherton, when we compared the water consumption for the first quarter of 1947 as against the same period for 1946, we found a 100% decrease. If the district office felt any compassion for the state of affairs revealed by our quite truthful explanation of "all toilets frozen solid this year", they failed to express it. By far the most effective explanation was to say, where the technicalities of plumbing permitted it, "increased rate of automatic flush in gents' toilet" or "decreased rate of automatic flush in gents' toilet" as circumstances required. No district office clerk that I ever met was foolhardy enough to risk asking for further information as to why these variations in the rate of flush had been thought to be necessary.

Gas also had its problems. Even after the 1939/45 war, many Black Country stations were still lit by gas, a result, we understood, of mutual pacts made between the railway and the gas companies nearly a century before. Staff clerks' store cupboards contained numerous boxes of mantles of various sizes. Not only was the office at Netherton lit entirely by gas, but so were the goods shed and canal shed. Electricity was only to be found in the cranes. Of these cranes, the 10-tonner had originally been 'mandraulic' and worked by four handles; but, keeping pace with the march of progress, it had recently been electrified. This invasion of its monopoly must have been resented by the gas, for when the crane rotated ('wombled') with any lift in excess of 5 tons, all the gas mantles used to break and out would go the lights. In the ensuing darkness a chorus of voices could be heard saying "I tode yer, day I?"

Apart from one light, the only gas at Blowers Green was a gas ring intended for boiling kettles but normally used only for lighting cigarettes when the staff were short of matches. I was, therefore, much puzzled when the district office complained of a 50% increase in gas consumption.

Investigation revealed that a new member of the staff, young Alfie the lad-numbertaker from Netherton working part time under the Blowers Green crane as a slinger, was heating a tin of Heinz beans on the gas ring every day for his dinner. He was allowing more than the full period of heating recommended by the makers on the tin; for, he said, he liked his dinner really hot. District office at Snow Hill, though they accepted my findings based unashamedly on these facts, were not, I felt, entirely pleased with the answer.

THE EAST GRINSTEAD CARRIAGE LIFT

The 'Carriage Lift' story was told to me 40+ years ago when I was a Relief Station Master and the "event" is probably early 1960s or, possibly, late 1950s.

It would appear that a new recruit had joined the diagramming office and had discovered a stock diagram for a London Bridge to East Grinstead Low Level service which reappeared after an hour or so on an East Grinstead High Level to London Bridge working. This intrigued our recruit to the point that he eventually plucked up sufficient courage to ask a colleague how the transfer from Low Level to High Level was achieved.

His colleague explained about the Armstrong Lift in the north sidings at Waterloo (W&C Stock entrance) and then explained that a similar device existed at East Grinstead to lift the carriages up from Low Level to High Level. The recruit accepted the explanation.

A few weeks later, curiosity got the better of the recruit so he caught a train to East Grinstead and knocked on the door of the Station Master's office. He duly introduced himself and asked if he might be able to see the carriage lift. The story ends here as no one seemed willing to repeat precisely what the Station Master said in response apart from showing the recruit the exit from the office.

John Lacy

EFFICIENCY

Thus far the LMS has been largely ignored, certainly not deliberately and whilst the tales related thus far have been deliberately referred to having occurred on the GWR or Southern, it is almost certain similar events occurred 'north of Euston'.

In describing the events one may be tempted to recall, no doubt with a wry smile, the circumstances as prevailed a few decades ago involving organisations like the GPO, gas-board and 'the electric'. As an example I recall the occasion when there was a definite smell of gas emanating from under the stairs - we looked (not with a naked flame) and decided the 'experts' should be called.

'You've got a leak said the man', 'You need a new meter, I will get one'. That was on the Monday.

On Tuesday a new meter was indeed delivered, but the men doing so advised they he just did the deliveries and not installations.

Wednesday a fitter arrived to swap the two meters - but his job was only to fit it, not to commission nor remove the old.

One of those task was completed the following day, I cannot recall in what order, but I do know it took five different men, five visits to remedy the fault, and of course we had to ensure there was somebody in every day for a week, 'Cannot tell you when it will be during the day', was the set telephone message. (But at least that was a human being and not an automated answering service…… .)

I suspect the reason for the (in)action was the sheer size of the gas board itself, meaning each task had to be pidgeon-holed and dealt with in a set fashion. Perhaps they had at their head someone who had once worked on the LMS….

The Station itself had grown up simply because of the presence of the junction. Names could be given here, but intentionally they are not. Especially as any serious student of the LMS will no doubt quickly identify the location for themselves.

Two platforms and a bay existed. The main buildings on one side and a footbridge linking the two. For years this had possessed a single creaking and rotten board, caused by a persistent drip from the gutter join on the roof above which meant water was blown back inside whenever the rain arrived from the west – which was of course most of the time.

The result was an accumulation of water running down the inside of the metal sidewalls leaving a rusty smear and collecting on the relevant floorboard. Time and time again the station master had requested the authorities repair the aforementioned area, but each time lack of time, resources, or other more urgent engagements prevailed. It was only when Lady Ponsonby-Smythe from the nearby manor house had almost slipped through upon her return from a shopping trip 'to Town' one evening, that at last the engineers agreed to a repair. And that was arranged for Monday next.

It practice it should have been a straightforward repair as well. Reports having been circulated as to what was needed, the station master even sending in the dimensions of the wooden board to be replaced. Dutifully a railway carpenter complete with bag of tools arrived on the down stopper, was greeted by the Station Master and immediately directed to where the repair was needed. Said artisan however, insisted that after all that travelling it was first time for his tea-break

After copious quantities of liquid had been consumed it was time for an inspection of the worksite. Measurements were taken, the whole recorded on a tattered piece of paper from a jacket pocket and then a further inspection viewed from trackside looking up from underneath. Thus far the time occupied had involved almost two hours, and the floorboard was still in the precarious state it had been at the start. The outcome was a few words of wisdom from the carpenter, "Needs a new bit of wood Guv, I'll get one sent down". And with that he made his way towards the waiting room on the up platform to await a train to take him back to his home station.

No amount of protestation did any good either.

'REBUILDING THE STATION, Great Bunting, Whimshire'.

'During the 1920s the Portersfoote Bunting Light Railway decided to rebuild its terminus at Great Bunting, widening the overall roofed station to accommodate two tracks, one of which was for undercover storage of rolling stock, The need for this was brought about by the collapse here of the carriage shed, which had been erected on poor foundations. The original 1869 stone station building was demolished and replaced with a less grandiose wood and corrugated iron structure, Stonework was donated to St. Basil's, the parish church, and used to construct a very tall spire on top of the existing tower, not without some misgivings in view of the wafer-thin foundations known to exist beneath this ancient edifice. All work was carried out simultaneously and without any interruption to normal train sendees, an organisational triumph indeed!'

©Peter Barnfield

STATION GARDENS

Something missing on the modern railway is the station garden. Where once windows boxes and neat borders adorned there are now plastic signs and concrete paving. Add to this the almost total lack of actual station staff – has anyone actually seen a Porter in the present millennia - indeed does the grade even exists today? (We do have 'Customer Assistants – staff who walk around with what appear to be a black and white 'ping-pong' bat, although I cannot be sure as to the latter's exact purpose. The suggestion as to some form of sadomasochism towards erring passengers - sorry customers - impossible to rule out.)

Years before, and regardless of the company involved, the route to promotion in most of the grades within the traffic department was via the platform and in consequence the station garden. Signalmen, foremen, station masters and inspectors would all bear witness to the early days of their career and the time when planting, weeding and tending were on par with the need to sweep out the offices, light the fires, and post the various notices. (Even to carry luggage sometimes!)

Having received a basic grounding (pardon the pun) sometimes such earthy activities would continue through later life on the railway, signal box gardens not unknown, nor the cultivation of certain salad vegetables within or in the immediate proximity to the signal box itself - the number of windows meaning many boxes possessed similar properties to that of a greenhouse and were thus ideal for the purpose.

Adrian Vaughan in his delightful rendition 'Signalman's Morning' recounts that in his own early days as a Porter at Challow how he was involved in the restoration of the station garden, something that was possible at a country station, but hardly plausible at locations like Bristol, Birmingham or Paddington, not withstanding the fact that at the latter the concourse was referred to as 'The Lawn'.

Having set the scene, and let us similarly not forget the veritable army of platelayers and gangers who rented pockets of land at the lineside to produce their own produce, we turn now to one particular branch line in the 1950s. Again names

are not important, suffice to say, various stations along this line had in years past been awarded certificates as well as a small cash prize in recognition of their annual displays. (Did you know for example that on the GWR there was even a 'railway nursery' based at Gloucester from which, for many years, bedding plants and annuals might be cultivated ready to be despatched to stations around the system.)

Our own country station had been the recipient of such prizes over the years, the once brightly coloured certificates having faded over the years yet still displayed in wooden frames within the confines of the booking office. Every one told its own story, 'First prize 1928, 1936 and 1937', small round stickers added to the original certificate to commemorate additional awards – the company were 'prudent', after all why issue a new certificate when the addition of a small piece of paper to a pre-existing award could serve the same purpose. In addition there were other, slightly less ornate awards, 'Second-Class', 'Highly-Commended' and the like, examples of when perhaps a late frost or un-seasonally rain heavy had put paid to what might surely have been an otherwise higher award, the tempest occurring on the days just before the anticipated inspection from the divisional office.

Regardless of the actual standard achieved there was always the trip to Paddington / Waterloo / Euston / Kings Cross for the issuing of the actual award certificate and with it a monetary token. To receive this it was the practice for the local Station Master and one of the Porters to travel in their 'No 1' uniform. The Station Master to take the credit of course, notwithstanding the fact his actual involvement would have been supervisory only (he might also be hoping to get noticed by the hierarchy) the Porter regarding it as a day out and a sop for all the hard work actually undertaken.

Come the time of the presentation the award was made to each representative in turn, flash-bulbs would crackle and a certificate and money changed hands. A few words would also be said, the Superintendent asking something like, "And what will you be doing for next year?", expecting a reply along the lines of how the borders might be enhanced or perhaps additional roses be planted.

It was prudent though not to give too much away, after all one's rivals might also be present, it sometimes difficult to compete with a neighbouring station who might have the advantage of habitual gifts of plants or blooms from a regular passenger. (In return donating passenger would no doubt receive what we might nowadays refer to as 5* treatment

'PLANTING BY STEAM, Portersfoote Bunting Light Railway'.

'Whimshire Composty is one of two little Jenny Wren brown engines allocated to the Horticultural Department of the PBLR. The department provides hanging baskets and flowers for the lineside and stations, also produce for the refreshment rooms. There are several mobile greenhouses, the one here being equipped with Adams' Steam Planting Apparatus and Wire Operated Watering Can, A disc and bar signal warns other trains that planting is in progress and timetables are adjusted or become flexible at certain times of the year to allow for delays. An arched gateway beside the engine shed at Portersfoote Bunting gives access to the walled gardens and potting sheds, where one of the locomotives is generally in steam throughout the winter, heating both the greenhouses and the manager's cottage nearby.'

whenever they travelled: after all it is not what you know but who you know.

Back at the presentation and after refreshments the various delegates would make their way back to the home station, the discussion on the return usually centring on how they might indeed attempt to beat their neighbours the following year. This then was the norm for many years, that is until one rather strong willed porter, possibly fortified with more liquid courage than was ideal, pronounced to his superior, "You buy begonias with your half of the money if you like, I did the b****y work so I knows what I'm doing with my half".

In many way this outward lack of respect for authority was no more than a sign of changing times and changing attitudes, no more so when years later after nationalisation and on the same line, the awards were still taking place but with a reduced staff – to suit a reduced passenger count. The gardens, the certificates, and the monetary award all similarly diminished.

So after passenger services had been withdrawn and the station survived on freight traffic only, the men were still encouraged to maintain the standards of years past although now the certificates simple read '……..Goods' as to the location.

Come what to be the final year of survival for the actual line in question and in early spring announcements were made as to the prizes awarded. Yet again our 'Goods' station was selected – although how such a judgement was actually made may be open to question, the once proud platform gardens overgrown whilst it was a long time since a window box had been cultivated. (Perhaps the visiting judge had some difficulty in identifying a flower from a weed.) Whatever, it was announced prizes would be awarded at a ceremony at a divisional location at the end of July, in itself a come down

from the days when such gatherings had been held in the metropolis.

With a reduced staff now it was just one man, the porter / signalman who ventured forth to the awards ceremony. On the stage were the great and the good, the hierarchy, managers and lesser mortals, plus representatives from the press – both railway and local. As the name of the respective location was called, so the delegate walked forth, up the steps at one end of the stage towards the dais where a rather portly manager waited with hand outstretched to welcome each and give out a certificate and wallet of money.

Somehow the whole ethos seemed outmoded, a link with the past, such a view enhanced by the age of those present, all in their 50s at least and many nearing retirement. These were the men who could indeed remember the past, their own start as 'Junior Gardeners' perhaps the official grade should have been 'Porter / Gardener'. It was noticeable too that the modern day managers, the ones straight from college and university were conspicuous by their absence, they having little regard for the traditions of the past – of which this was of course one.

Our man walked slowly towards the centre of stage, arriving to take in his hand the given items, "And how will you use the award towards next year?" asked the donor (exactly the same question as might have been asked years past). "Not on the railway", our recipient answered at the same time glancing around. No one had ever dared respond in such fashion before. He quickly continued, "You are closing our line in two weeks time and making me redundant". A deathly silence befell. There was nothing that could be said, instead 100 or so heads tuned to watch the back of a proud man who had given his working life to 'the company' walk with head high towards the door. He did not wait for the refreshments, the certificate found a place at his home – along with cuttings from the roses that had once adorned the goods shed.

CATS

I have been told that in Scotland the railways employed a few official dogs which were used by the permanent way gangers to evict sheep from railway land. Some railway police also used dogs to reinforce their authority. But that was as far as the dogs got.

Cats, however, were quite another matter. It was a poor station or depot that had no cat on the establishment, official or unofficial: most had more than one. Kidderminster, for instance, had three: one in the refreshments rooms, one in the grain shed, and one based on the goods office. All three were lady cats, and all three shared the same husband, a doughty ginger torn who belonged to the local butcher at the end of the station drive. Their combined output of tortoiseshell and ginger kittens was prodigious and much in demand.

The Great Western was prepared to pay a salary to established cats based on the milk index. To qualify for an established cat, the station had to include a store for foodstuffs or things likely to take the fancy of rats and mice. The milk index meant that their salary was based on the cost of one pint of milk per cat per week, and was paid out of petty cash against a written receipt from whoever was acting as the cat's amanuensis. Needless to say, this official contribution covered only a fraction of the real cost per week: railway cats were expected to do for themselves well. The difference was met by the cat's curator supplemented by generous gifts in kind from other members of the staff.

The first two railway cats that I met were at Chippenham in 1938. They were employed to police the grain warehouse and did so with such verve and elan that their pitch must have been marked as a no-go area on the pocket map of every local rat or mouse. Having got things up to standard, these two tabbies had a system which ensured that everything stayed that way.

This was how they worked it. There was a roadway between the nearest railway line and the narrow platform on to which the doors of the warehouse opened. When a wagon was being unloaded, a plank bridge was erected over the gap between the wagon and the platform, supported by a trestle in the middle. Over this bridge the incoming sacks of cattle feed were wheeled on barrows one at a time. The two cats positioned themselves, one on either side of the platform end of the bridge, like two officials at Heathrow checking the out-turn of a dubious flight from Tangier. Each time that he passed between them,

"...fourteen before midnight...lined up...for our inspection".

From 'Behind the Lines' by Christopher Burton.

the porter stopped his barrow for the cats to check for any stowaway mice in the sack. If they held up a paw, or mewed, the porter said, he put the sack on one side for further examination.

Felix was the shed cat at Hockley. He had been born and spent his kittenhood at Soho and Winson Green, but had blotted his copybook in the eyes of the staff who used to feed him by catching too many young birds, So they decided to deport him in a covered van that was going to Hockley. The hours he had spent confined in the van had done little to improve Felix's temper, so, when he stepped out on to the goods shed platform at Hockley, he scowled at his rescuers and made it quite clear that he would not tolerate any liberties being taken with him. He did, however, accept a saucer of milk offered by the railway police and decided to stay.

No one could have described Felix as a feline 'preux chevalier'. He was a hard-boiled twenty-minute-egg of a cat. Had he been born a human, he would have been of the two-gun Jake type, spoken out of the side of his mouth, and spat loudly into the saw dust. Personal hygiene, sad to say, came low in his list of priorities, and though his mother would have described him as white, he went through life a drab shade of grey.

But as a catcher of rats he was superb: mice he disdained as only fit for kittens. It was a regular sight on night shifts to see Felix go by with a huge rat in his mouth; one special evening he caught fourteen before midnight and lined up their remains for our inspection. His relations with the staff were on a strictly business footing: if he wanted something moved so that he could get behind it, he would enlist the help of anyone who was near. Only the railway police, perhaps because of that first saucer of milk, were allowed to see the warmer side of his nature. With them he was on almost affectionate terms, and it was they who used to take him in the police car down to the vet for the many repairs that were needed.

Charlie at Spinners End, Old Hill, was quite a different character. His mother had been station cat before him, and when she passed on he took over the job. To him the three most important things in life were the ladies, food, and the office stove. His prowess with the ladies was legendary in Spinners End; he expected food to be provided on a lavish scale, and was not disappointed; in front of the stove he would sit digesting the food and planning the night's amatory excursions.

Then in 1964 a final ripple of the big splash caused by Dr. Beeching reached the Black Country; Spinners End was closed and Charlie was made redundant. Although offered the vacant post of station cat at nearby Cradley Heath, he refused to accept it, walking back to Spinners End in the first 24 hours. Offers of private accommodation met with the same response: Charlie just walked home again. So when Spinners End's last day of life arrived, Charlie was still there. The office had been stripped of all its furniture; only the stove remained with Charlie sat in front of it. Before we locked the door for the last time, the depot clerk picked up Charlie and set him down outside on the doorstep. Looking back as we drove away, we could see him still sitting there, a sad black figure.

A motor driver who worked for one of the coal merchants at Spinners End had long been a friend and admirer of Charlie. This worthy man took on the job of feeding him: they met punctually at the locked station gate at eight o'clock each morning when the rations for the day were passed through the wooden slats. At last, after some weeks of this procedure, Charlie was persuaded to transfer to Cradley Heath, much to the relief of all his friends.

Minnie was the goods office cat at Kidderminster. A handsome tabby, she was sometimes short tempered; so much so that strangers who wished to stroke her were advised to do so with a rolled up newspaper. She was a cat with a strong sense of propriety; so, when a litter of kittens was expected, she made arrangements for the actual accouchement to take place in the privacy of the little hut where the ganger kept his tools. Then, after their eyes were open, she carried the kittens one at a time in her mouth from the hut to the office where she deposited them at the bottom of a large wicker waste paper basket.

It was one of Minnie's kittens who, like many a railway cat, made an involuntary journey by rail. This kitten had been slow to find a home and was getting quite large; so large that she and Minnie had started to quarrel, as mothers and teenage daughters will. There must have been a mouse, or some attractive smell, in the wagon being loaded to Stockton-on-Tees for the men had twice ejected the inquisitive kitten from it. Next morning she could not be found. The day after that Stockton-on-Tees came on the phone to say were we short of a cat? If so, they said, they would either send it back or keep it themselves. Knowing Minnie's views on the subject of her daughter, we asked Stockton to keep her.

We had two similar cases in the Black Country. Wolverhampton's cat made a trip to Weymouth and was sent back in a beautifully fitted tea chest with a special cushion in the bottom for her to sleep on. One of our West Bromwich cats landed up at Bricklayers Arms. The Southern men, on being told over the phone that we would like her back, packed her in a specially adapted gin crate; carted her across London to Paddington, and put her on the train to Snow Hill. There she was met by a helpful inspector and put on the 'stopper' to West Bromwich. Released from her crate, she walked over to her usual saucer, which was empty, and made it quite clear that, after her long journey, she could do with a drink.

I should like to have met a remarkable cat who, I was told, lived in the triangle between the lines at Gloucester Road where the line to Earls Court leaves the Inner Circle. To get anywhere, this cat had to cross several sets of live rails. But never once did she put a paw on the wrong rail, and taught her many kittens to do the same. You can imagine her lecturing the kittens something like this:- "Now, children, remember you can tread on that one and that one; but not that one. And look right before you cross this line; and left before you cross that."

From 'Behind the Lines' by Christopher Burton.

COMMON USER WAGONS

So what do the initials 'L.M.S.' stand for? Answer, "One 'ell of a mess". Certainly that would be true at Sutton Harbour, Plymouth on Monday 31 January 1948. (Not Friday the 13th you will notice.)

We may even be reminded of the delightful Rev. Wilbur Audrey's 'troublesome trucks' characters, perhaps LMS open No. 93214 was the original 'roll-model' - this time the pun is intended.

Whatever, this particular 'common-user' vehicle, and meaning a standard wagon that might be used anywhere in the UK notwithstanding the fact that it belonged to the LMS (similar 'common-user' vehicles were on the books of the GWR, SR and LNER) found itself legitimately on the edge of the wharf at Sutton Harbour on that fateful day. Running parallel to the edge of the waterline was a single line of rails accessed by one of two wagon turntables. A stop block was provided at only at one end of this single line of rails.

For reasons that are not reported, No 93214 rebounded off this stop block and with the nearest wagon turntable set other than exactly parallel with the rails deposited itself first on the quayside before taking a nose dive into the harbour. Whether it was waiting to be loaded / unloaded is not known.

Recovery involved lashing empty oil drums to the chassis after which it was towed back to the foreshore - presumably later retuned to its owners but in "One 'ell of a mess".

'The Boat Train, Tawnyport Pier & Rly Coy'.

Unable to afford a bridge, this impoverished Company has instead converted the steam launch 'Tempest' to ferry trains across the river. Somewhat unstable in rough weather, the 'Tempest' can only operate when a tide is favourable and passengers must distribute themselves evenly throughout the carriages to minimise the risk of capsize. In accordance with the amendment to the Company's Rule Book following the sinking of the locomotive 'Prospero', 'Miarnda' is firmly teathered to a bollard before attempting to couple up to the carriages'.

RECRUITING

It always seemed to me that we either had too few staff on the railway or too many; never just right. One week you would be rebuked by the district office for sloth in recruiting (they even encouraged the staff to ask their wives to work part time); the next Monday into your office would file three gentlemen, with brief cases and sombre expression, announcing that they had come to investigate your staff establishment with a view to substantial reductions.

A month later, after pruning the lad-porter's overtime, they would move on to spread their sweetness and light elsewhere.

Recruiting was not easy: in those days of full employment, good men and women were hard to come by, and, compared with industry in Birmingham and the Black Country, our wage levels were far too low - or theirs were far too high. It is not often that one thinks of the right retort at the right moment; usually it is when you get home at night. However, when representing the GWR at a well-attended meeting of the Birmingham Junior Chamber of Commerce, I was asked petulantly by a sleek young executive from the motor industry why his commuter train had failed to run that morning. "Probably," I said, "because you have just offered the driver twice as much a week to come and sweep out your canteen."

We learnt from experience not to waste time describing the job until the applicant had first had a look at the wage scales. Then, often with comments that made the girls in the office blush, they upped and went.

Two applicants stand out in my memory. The first came for a job at West Bromwich. He was a quiet-looking chap and, undeterred by the wage scales, proceeded to fill out the application form. This form contained all the usual questions - age, past experience, and so on - including one towards the end which asked if the applicant had ever been convicted by the courts, and, if so, for what. A modest little space was provided for the reply. This applicant penned busily in this space and then asked what he ought to do when there was not enough room on the form for all that he wanted to write. The staff clerk gave him a piece of foolscap and, looking over his shoulder, was horrified to see him filling half the sheet with previous convictions, nearly all of which were for theft. We were so impressed by his exhibition of truthfulness that we were ready to risk taking him on: but district office said no.

The other applied for a job at Coventry. He was a huge man with a fierce dark jowl, a cross between Bill Sykes and King Kong. He had had six different jobs in the last six months. In the 'Reason for leaving' column, instead of the usual 'Money no good', he had written 'Couldn't get on with the gaffer'. This remark he had dittoed down the column against the other five. I decided that it would not be prudent to add to our existing stock of people with this distressing disability.

After their probationary service, all candidates for what was called 'appointment' were obliged to produce two testimonials from suitable worthies such as the vicar, doctor, teacher, local councilor, or someone of alleged note in local trade and industry. Obtaining these was not always easy: one of my porters at Blowers Green, who was a comparative stranger to the area, drew blank at all the usual sources. The district office at Snow Hill enquired twice why no testimonials were forthcoming, hinting the second time that perhaps the man (or we) had something to hide. The fact that he had been working for us for six months steadily and well was, they said, irrelevant.

The episode ended happily however. In the yard were two coal merchants, the numbers of whose coal wagons this lad inscribed in a notebook each morning. Noticing that the lad's usual happy smile was missing, they asked the reason and were told of his plight. Ten minutes later he returned to the office with two write-ups couched in such glowing terms that; as the foreman remarked, they would have got him into heaven, let alone the GWR.

The West Indian fraternity had trouble over testimonials right from the start. At West Bromwich one excellent motor-driver from Jamaica produced a most impressive document with a picture of a banana tree in the top right hand corner and a eulogy - presumably by the owner of the banana tree -

which said, inter alia, that he was a good beavin man.

"What," I asked the staff clerk, "does 'beavin' mean?" He did not know; nor did the foreman; nor the chief clerk. If we sent the thing off to district office, they were sure to write back and ask us to clarify the meaning of this word. A suggestion that it meant beavering or working hard like a beaver found little support; if he had come from Canada, possibly; from Jamaica, no.

The correct answer was provided by a highly intelligent South African Cape Malay. "Beavin," he said, "means behaving - a good behaving man, see?"

Some half a century after they started work as juniors, retiring railwaymen are given their testimonials back. These, written with neat pothooks on faded yellow paper by some long departed teacher, paint a picture that it is hard to reconcile with the bald and paunchy sixty-five year old who is being asked to sign for them. "I have known John Smith," say the pothooks, "since he started at this school. He has always been a clean, alert, and trustworthy boy....." It would be going a bit far to claim that all boys were the 'fathers of the men': but a lot of them were - quite enough to explain the 'Great' in Great Western Railway.

From 'Behind the Lines' by Christopher Burton.

CONTROL

The word control is a term probably little known other than to railwaymen and actual followers of railway operation. In reality 'control' was where all the problems involved in the actual operation of the railway were dealt with. Had the system operated exactly as per the working timetable then in theory at least, controllers would not have been necessary, but add into the melting pot, delays, breakdowns, extra trains required to be run at short notice, crews arriving late so missing a booked turn, or requiring relief, and some idea of the work (and stress) involved may be glimpsed at.

Looking back it is quite amazing how the actual running of the railway was accomplished in what was a pre-computer age, the sole technical assistance being a bank of telephones.

Running the operation would be a Chief Controller, followed by lesser mortals and then, at the sharp end, the actual controllers themselves, the number of these dependent upon the geographical area plus the intensity of the train service. It followed that the number of staff on duty at night would be less than during the day, similarly one office might cover miles of branch and cross-country routes combined, compared with a restricted geographical area within a metropolitan conurbation. Wow-betide also any man 'on the ground' who defied control, those giving the instructions were invariably senior railwaymen, sometimes ex signalmen or inspectors, used to making routing and traffic decisions on the spot and whose combined length of service was invariably greater than the time railways had actually been in operation.

How these controllers kept abreast what was occurring on their patch was by information passed to them from specific points. One signal box might have to notify the control office of the passing times of all freight workings, another all main line passenger trains / inter regional (company) services and the like. (The task of informing control usually delegated to the booking lad in the respective signal box.) In this way the men receiving the information could plot the running of various key workings and were thus able to instruct other signal boxes to perhaps, hold, run, or sidetrack a specific service in order to minimise disruption or prioritise a service – a boat train for example.

A key requirement also was for the controller to have a encyclopaedic knowledge of his patch, how long it would take for a freight to run between 'A' and 'B'. the capacity of a station loop, and whether the timetable allowed for so and so sidings to be empty at a set time of day – and how long before they might be needed for another working.

So railway knowledge was essential, but so was a little bit of knowledge beyond true timetabling and operation as well. Take the occasion when one particular controller who had a penchant for gambling would telephone the terminus at the end of a particular branch line ostensibly to enquire as to the running of the branch line service but in reality to enquire as to what horses were being loaded that day. His logic being that the trainers would not be sending expensive horses any distance if they did not have a reasonable chance of winning. Reasoned logic yes, except for one slight problem, the bookie he used drove a up-market car, our poor controller never ventured beyond a bone-shaker of a bicycle.

There were other advantages of being in control as well, arranging prompt delivery of one's own goods an example, being able to arrange for ones railway employee relatives to finish at a respectable time when a social function had been arranged and perhaps most sly of all, to enquire as to the behaviour of a son-in-law whose excuse that he was always required to work overtime was beginning to wear thin.

Nowadays control and signal box operation is sometimes combined. The sphere of operation of one panel so great that decisions can often be taken on the spot. Unfortunately with the centralising of operating so came the demise of individuality, and even if a branch line does exists somewhere at the end of which there are racing stables, that terminus will no doubt be unstaffed and the horses taken to their respective meets by road.

'THE CONTROLLER'S OFFICE'

Friday the 13 would appear to be living up to its reputation, judging by the controller's chalk board with its list of delays etc. Has the railwayman at the door arrived to announce further bad news or has someone found the missing 1,13pm Bradforde Longflap railcar, one wonders?

Not particularly efficient at operating trains, the Portersfoote Bunting Light Railway also has a problem in the paperwork department, although the chief clerk is something of an expert when it comes to the Whimshire Gazette crossword, The fact that only one of the battery of timepieces seems to be functioning need not worry one unduly, however, since the area served by the railway has always ignored GMT preferring local time, as governed by the church clock which is clearly visible from the station platform,

NAGS

It is a common saying, particularly among retired railwaymen who think that they know best, that the railways provided a better service to the public with steam and horses than they do today with electricity, diesel, power boxes, and computers.

But at the time when the horses were still working we did not look on them as economic factors, but rather as pleasant things to have about the place. Indeed, one gaffer at Wolverhampton (Herbert St), realising that his ten horses were being out-performed by the motors in the town centre and thus were in danger of redundancy, used statistics to prolong their life.

An inveterate nose-patter and sugar-provider himself, he knew that the horses would be judged by the average weight carted per horse per week, so he took the most powerful horse off the town and put him on carting pig iron instead which jacked up the average per horse nicely and saved the day for the time being.

If only it had been possible to turn the horses off with an ignition key at the end of the week and re-activate them by the same means on Monday morning, they would be working still. But their Sunday dinners and welfare meant Sunday work for the stablemen at Sunday rates of pay, and, cost-wise, counted cruelly against them.

From 'Behind the Lines'
by
Christopher Burton.

Like the rest of the staff who worked with them, the horses were individuals. No two were exactly alike. There were the morose and ill-tempered ones whose ears went back quickly and the whites of their eyes showed. Their teeth were quite ready to test the strength of the blue serge that covered the arms and posteriors of any unwary company servants standing in the vicinity.

Such a horse was Fred at Birkenhead who weighed over a ton: to take him out into the town tended to be bad for public relations, so his duties were confined to the depot, mainly shunting. At this he was an expert. He would throw his weight into the collar to get the wagon moving, accelerate away, and then, when the wagon was rolling nicely, step to one side and stop so that the chain dropped off. The shunters used to assert, to anyone who would believe them, that he looked at the wagon labels to see how hard a pull was required.

Still at Birkenhead, was Bill - a one-man horse. The one man in Bill's case was a scruffy little carter whose time-keeping left a lot to be desired. To teach him the error of his ways, the foreman took him off driving and used him for mucking out in the stables in the hope that the pungent environment would speed the process of penitence and reformation. Bill in the meanwhile went off over the ferry to Liverpool with a relief carter.

About mid-morning there was a telephone call from the Liverpool police. One of our horse drays, they said, was causing an obstruction in the docks as the horse refused to move. It was Bill. Admitting defeat, the foreman sent the little carter over to Liverpool. When he arrived on the scene, as well as waiting traffic, there was a crowd of onlookers, police, and, in the middle of it all, Bill with his ears back. While still some distance away, the little carter called out "Bill! What's the matter?" and Bill's ears pricked up. He elbowed his way through the crowd and took Bill's head. As they clip-clopped happily away, the carter addressed the gathering over his shoulder. "It's quite easy," he said, "if you happen to know how to do it."

Another characteristic of the horses was their greed. If they had known about Rule 3 (ii) in the GWR Rule Book which expressly forbade the soliciting of gratuities, they would have denied that it applied to them. One Wolverhampton horse distinguished himself by gently extracting a french roll from the shopping bag of a lady standing in a bus queue without her knowing. He also made a scene outside a cake shop where he was usually given a stale doughnut. Thinking that his carter had been an unconscionably long time in coming out with the elevenses, he took his cart over the wide pavement and was only prevented from going into the shop by the shafts sticking in the doorway. His head, however, was far enough into the shop for him to be able to sniff at the loaded shelves and make greedy noises. Nor would he back out until all his demands had been fully met.

The carters, who grew extremely fond of their horses (and, of course, vice versa), used to say that they could almost talk.

This was certainly true at Hockley during the animals' midday break. There would be a row of them having their nosebags (the horses as well as the carters) while their carts were backed up to the platform for loading or unloading. But a careless toss of the head could cause the nosebag to slip down the diner's neck to where he or she could not reach it.

The imploring looks that they then directed at passers-by to help them out of this predicament were more than human.

One day at Kidderminster I was talking to the checker in the weighbridge when the face of a small girl appeared above the window sill; a finger tapped on the glass. Outside was a diminutive girl leading with a halter an even more diminutive Shetland pony, not much more than eight hands high. We asked what we could do to help.

"Will you please weigh my pony", said the girl; "but you must not tell anybody what it is as they've got to guess his weight at the fete tomorrow".

We stood the tiny pony in the middle of the plate and weighed him with great ceremony, handing over an official railway memo reinforced with the imprint of the station rubber stamp - all for free. The girl thanked us prettily and the pair set off down Comberton Hill. Before she had gone many yards, however, she turned and came back, still leading the pony. She fixed us with a threatening frown. "You won't tell anyone, will you?" she said.

FOREMEN

"Old Jack', chief foreman at Wolverhampton (Herbert Street) pointed to his gold braided hat. "In this job", he said, " you need to have the eyes of a hawk and also to be as blind as a bat. The skill in the job is knowing when to be which."

A very profound remark. But 'Old Jack' was a fine foreman, built on stoutly traditional lines, with white hair and a knowing twinkle in his eyes.

In addition to 'Old Jack', Julius Caesar would have approved of four out of five Great Western foremen; for those with a lean and hungry look were rare. 'Tiny', our cartage foreman at Great Bridge, when first measured for his uniform, turned in figures for his vital statistics of 44", 45", 46". Whether it was that foremen put it on after they were appointed, or whether they owed their promotion to their circumference, was always a subject of debate.

This portliness of stature had its disadvantages. In the early 1950s, British Railways eager to show how up-to-date they were in modern industrial practice, inaugurated an ambitious scheme for Training Within Industry - or TWI. All gaffers, clerks in charge of other clerks, and foremen were to be processed. For the gaffers and clerks in Birmingham a series of classes was established at Snow Hill with a smart lecturer from Paddington in charge: for the foremen another class was assembled at Hockley under an inspector. They came to be known as 'Snow Hill Grammar' and 'Hockley Secondary Mod'.

The task of the inspector at Hockley was a daunting one. Facing him, and seated on hard wooden benches, were about fifteen venerable gentlemen whose combined years of service added up to some six centuries of railway experience.

The attitude of the class was passively hostile, slightly mollified in those cases where the pupil was on overtime.

The inspector prudently explained that he was not there to teach them their jobs, but to teach them how to teach others. Silence. He would begin, said the inspector, by teaching them how to tie an electrician's knot, so that they could see what correct teaching methods were. Short pieces of wire were distributed round the benches.

The class rebelled. Why, it asked, if it had got to submit to this nonsense, could it not be taught something to do with railways? It pointed out that even if it ever did need to tie an electrician's knot, the union would not allow it. Foolishly, it suggested folding ('lapping') up a traffic sheet. The inspector agreed.

After some delay said item was purloined and eventually brought into the room by two sweating goods porters. The new sheet opened out on the floor at the back of the room: it was stiff, and smelly.

The inspector, glancing round the room, selected the two fattest individuals available. Those who have ever done it know only too well that folding up a traffic sheet is a job that requires a lot of bending down. Beset by bulging waistcoats in front and lumbago in the rear, the two victims struggled through the performance. Any amusement the rest of the class may have felt was clouded by the thought that they would be asked to do it next. They were; two by two until all had had a go. After the dinner break, a motion that they would like to know more about electricians' knots was carried unanimously.

Whether the foremen who left Hockley Secondary Mod were better men than when they came in was hard to prove. However you looked at it, their jobs, particularly in the Black Country, were far from easy. Sandwiched between the gaffers above and the men below, they had to deal with everything from compiling the weekly rosters for the staff to finding good homes for the station cat's surplus kittens. Some signed 'examine load' labels for anything up to ten anchors; they smoothed the ruffled feathers of angry coal jaggers, or put the same jaggers' wagons of coal out of position until they had paid their demurrage; many controlled the shunting engines, looked after the cartage, and dealt valiantly with all the stupid questions that polluted the ear-pieces of their telephones.

At local departmental committee meetings, the foremen had to sit with their gaffers, ready to argue the toss about tonnage bonus, working hours, trip working, or why the gas pressure was so low in the weighbridge.

One of the stock questions put to applicants at interviews for foremens' jobs was what would they do when confronted with a man who had refused to do what he was told. The answers to this question varied but, with really good foremen, the question never arose. A combination of personality, experience, and humour were worth a hundred rule books.

...'at some preposterous time in the small hours'....

BOLSHIE BORIS OF BRISTOL

Think of Bristol as a railway location and it would be surprising not to have the GWR station at Temple Meads uppermost in mind. True the majority of trains, facilities and therefore staff employed at Bristol were indeed Great Western and later Western Region men, but do not forget those from that other railway whose services regularly arrived and departed from that great city, the men who worked for the Midland Railway, later the LMS and eventually the London Midland Region whose own station was at St Phillips.

One of these men, and the time period will deliberately not be mentioned but may become apparent from what follows, was Boris. Born had been brought up in England although his Germanic sounding name meant he was the but of fun for some and for the same reason ignored by others. Over time this behaviour become more of a trial, something he was unable to deal with. Consequently he became ever more withdrawn, irritable and difficult to his colleagues. It was not therefore surprising he gained the nickname of 'Bolshie Boris'.

To be fair part of this behaviour was been brought on by himself, for not only did he perceive he was a laughing stock to his Midland colleagues but also to those who knew him and who worked for the Western - animosity between the employees of the two systems heightened as some of the Midland men had the distinct impression that when it came to wages and conditions of service the Western staff were far better off for undertaking similar work. Whether this was actually true is open to debate, suffice to say once the opposition learnt of the jealousy they were quick to exploit it.

Now friendly rivalry, name pulling and even practical jokes were all part of the general workaday behaviour amongst the men but the attitude of Boris was beginning to wear thin. He had become a man few wished to be involved with if they could, his revenge to anyone he perceived to be threatening was swift and even at times violent, soda in the tea, stolen sandwiches, deliberately switched labels on packages, and hidden workaday essential items all part of his repartee. Any one of these might have been expected to have resulted in the sack but nothing was ever definitely proven although there were many suspicions. The whole situation therefore ran the risk of disrupting the core business of running the railway at Bristol.

These matters had been known to the foreman for some time, but on the basis that most spats of this type will eventually sought themselves out, he was content to ignore the situation for as long as possible. But unfortunately the relationship between Boris and his colleagues did not improve and it was therefore time for the foreman to take action.

Now foreman achieve their grade through dint of work, experience and often guile. An ability to think problems through, maintain a knowledge of all they are responsible for and perhaps most important of all, to command the respect of the men they supervise. Our foreman was just such a man, who after considering the situation for a time devised a plan which, if successful, would teach Boris a lesson relative to his practical jokes although at the same time said foreman would also be having stern words with the rest of the workforce as to their own behaviour. He could do less as regards the Western men, although a word in the ear of his opposite number might do some good. Most important, if successful, his own men might become a bit more supportive of Boris so leaving him to feel less isolated.

But every plan or action needs careful planning, there would be just one opportunity and he had to bide his time until that opportunity arose.

It started with a few discreet enquiries as to the whereabouts of a particular type of railway vehicle. Now the railway system had numerous types of vehicles all designed for specific tasks. Passenger carriages of course and in turn sub-divided into brakes, composites, restaurant cars, first class etc. On the goods side there were open wagons, closed wagons, bolster wagons, cattle wagons, tanks etc., and in between the two came the various vans for mails, parcels and such like. Some of the latter were multipurpose, parcels on one day, pigeons the next and perhaps even baskets or punnets of fruit after that. The hygiene issue of which society has nowadays become so self-obsessed would never allow any such mixture today, perhaps it would have been frowned upon even then, but was probably conducted on the basis of, 'what the eye does not see….'.

We digress, for to return to the topic of railway vehicles, interspersed between all these types of vehicle were the really specialist vehicles, designed for one purpose only, and one of these was a corpse van. Here the use was obvious, the most regular traffic of this type some distance to the east, trains run by the South Western and the Southern on behalf of the London Necropolis Company from their own station at Waterloo to the cemetery at Brookwood - a single tickets for the principal and returns for the entourage.

It took some time, but eventually a corpse van was located and through calling in a few favours it was arranged to be worked to the loading point at the former Midland terminus at St Phillips.

But before this could happen the help of other individuals and staff was required, including that of a local undertaker.

Digressing again, the very fact that such things as corpse or hearse vans existed indicated a need. For many years coffins were placed in the guards compartment of trains, but where the deceased and or their family were well-to-do, and/or to avoid transhipping a coffin several times from point of departure to destination station, it was sometimes more appropriate to utilise a dedicated vehicle. Neither was this the first time such traffic had been handled at Bristol, not common but certainly not unknown, so it was hoped Boris would not be fooled by the ruse before it started.

And how it started was the day before, when before going off duty the foreman 'happened' to bump into Boris and advise him to be smart the next day as he had a special duty for him, and that he had been especially selected.

Here the foreman was being crafty, playing to his ego as well as making sure Boris would be present.

Come the next morning Boris presented himself as requested. He was told to make his way to a certain undertakers where, due to that organisations own internal difficulties, he would be acting as accompaniment to a coffin to be brought to the station where a hearse van was waiting. The foreman could of course have used an ordinary vehicle for the purpose but the fact a special duty van was present added credence to the story. Before this he was to ensure the interior of the van was tidy and presentable.

Having completed the latter task, Boris made his way

through the streets to the chapel of rest. Here he introduced himself and was informed the coffin contained the body of a late departed VIP, hence the importance of ensuring there was a 'presence' on the hearse. The undertaker apologised for having to ask the railway for help but all his men were occupied with other funerals on that day. Said undertaker was of course already in on the act, as was at least one other member of staff, of which more anon.

Boris was led to the waiting horse carriage upon which a coffin had been placed. It never occurred to him to think it strange that for a VIP a glass sided carriage was not being used. Fate also favours those who help themselves for the day was windy.

Boris climbed up alongside and they set off. It was a journey of a mile or so from the funeral parlour to the station during which time Boris began to imagine he could hear groaning coming from behind. He questioned this, only to be told it was first the weather, then his imagination and finally the fact that corpses as they decompose will fill with gas and in consequence sometimes noise results.

It was an only partly reassured Boris who arrived with the undertaker at the loading platform. His final job would be to assist in transporting the coffin into the van, but as he did so he was even more certain there were noises coming from within. He dared not question any further but was looking forward to when the task might be over.

As they lowered the coffin onto the floor of the van, the undertaker announced, 'I will be back in a moment - must relieve myself - you start securing it and I will be back to check in a moment'. Boris was therefore left alone, he was now convinced there were noises coming from within, not just any noise either, but creaking, groaning and even an occasional moan. He would be glad when the job was finished, but as he busied himself so the lid slowly rose in front of him and a voice announced, "I'm rather hungry , have you anything to eat?"

He was out and running in a flash, only to notice his work colleagues had suddenly appeared as if from nowhere complete with a laughing foreman. A few carefully chosen words in his ear and it was a new Boris who emerged, friend to all and equally respected in return.

LIGHT RAILWAYS - 1

Leaving apart the wonderful Listowel & Ballybunion line, which has already featured in these pages, perhaps the strangest railway business ever to operate in the British Isles has to be those lines managed by Col Holman Fred Stephens.

From Kent to Cornwall and from Somerset to Derbyshire, not forgetting in Wales, the Colonel had interests in varying lines, his being the archetypal 'Light Railway', represented today by the Kent & East Sussex whose unique charm is equally different to other preserved lines – all of course delightful in their own way.

'LUNCHTIME AT SEPIA FOLIATE, *Portersfoote Bunting Light Railway, Whimshire*'

'The PBLR passenger terminus at Sepia Foliate on the branch from Portersfoote Bunting, with railcars Ant & Aphid waiting at the platform. The crew brew tea using their kettle on Aphid's heat exchanger fitted to the exhaust pipe, while the station porter waters the railcar roof garden and the station cat awaits her chance to grab a sardine sandwich. Dianthus passes with some empty wagons bound for the Vermilion Mines on along the mineral extension.'

©*Peter Barnfield*

On the basis that 'any similarity is entirely coincidental', the accompanying images by Peter Barnfield create a delightful symmetry with that bygone age, the words being left to Peter to describe his own work.

'TESTING A BRIDGE, Portersfoote Bunting Light Rly., Whimshire'

'The infamous Bladderwort Bridge, constructed in 1881 for the extension of the line to Whiminster, has always been treated with the utmost suspicion by visiting inspectors dedicated to the cause of public safety. An annual inspection, using at least three locomotives to test for excessive deflection, is a feature of the railway calendar and on this occasion a truckload of housebricks has been added for good measure!'

©Peter Barnfield

INSPECTORS

District and divisional inspectors were a vital part in the railway set-up: and, broadly speaking, they corresponded to warrant officers in the Services - chief petty officers, sergeant-majors, and the like. Although issued with peaked caps, they seldom wore them, preferring instead 'Anthony Edens' or dark trilby types. Also essential were dark mackintoshes which they used to wear winter and summer alike. To the district gaffer, they were not only extensions to his strong right arm, enabling him to keep his flock of stations on the straight and narrow way of railway probity, but also his eyes, ears, and nose to uncover those stations who had left undone those things that they ought to have done, and similarly done those things that they ought not to have done.

No wonder, therefore, that the stations - particularly those with guilty consciences - viewed the visits and prying eyes of a visiting inspector with defensive foreboding. To them the movements of an inspector resembled those of an angry wasp flying round a classroom full of boys whose anxious eyes followed it round to see where it was going to land and possibly sting. An inspectors sting could in the form of an adverse report that went straight to the desk of the big gaffer at Snow Hill, Bristol, Worcester, and the like. In fairness to the inspectors, they did usually discuss their findings with the stationmaster or goods agent before they left, but, even if abject penitence was expressed, it did not often stave off the wrath to come.

However, there were some options open to stations to counter the danger. Forewarned was forearmed. Thus there had developed from time immemorial an intelligence network which could give advance notice of any official visitor who might upset what the poet Gray called the 'cool sequestered vale of life' at the station. The system was based on detailed observations at stations, plus a liberal use of the telephone.

Just before the War, I was accompanying an inspector from Swansea on what was supposed to be a surprise visit to Newcastle Emlyn in deepest West Wales. We arrived to find the stationmaster positioned on the platform exactly opposite the door of our compartment - a credit to the accuracy of his informant up the line at Llandyssul or Pencader. The stationmaster bowed politely and took us to his office where a pot of tea and three cups were already on the table.

Sometimes it could be managed without the telephone. One morning at Netherton I received from Snow Hill a nasty

...'where a pot of tea and three cups were already on the table'.

From 'Behind the Lines' by Christopher Burton.

letter asking why a new 15 ton mineral wagon was being allowed to stand empty and idle in Cox's Lane sidings on the line from Dudley to Old Hill. Cox's Lane was part of my little empire, and, as it happened, I knew all about the offending wagon. Also, I already knew that the chief inspector had been on the train from Dudley to Old Hill two days before, as my foreman at Blowers Green, who was psychic where inspectors were concerned, had seen his profile and black hat through the carriage window as the train went by. So I wrote back explaining that the wagon was a cripple, waiting for new axle brasses, and went on to say that had the chief inspector, instead of making his observations through the carriage window, got out and looked for himself, he would have seen the red card. There was no reply from Snow Hill, but I heard later from well placed contacts that the chiefs opinion of our counter-espionage system had gone up considerably.

Some lucky stations had a built-in immunity from inspectors' strictures. For instance, if the visiting inspector had himself been a foreman at that station before his elevation to the peerage, all the station had to say in answer to his probing questions was 'Same as when you were here, Ted' and leave it at that. Or As occurred at Spinners End, Old Hill. Here they may not have known everything, but they did know how to load a 5 ton mud anchor with a long stock into a seven-plank open wagon. One day they were just about to do so when a brash new inspector arrived saying that he was going to load it. After inviting him to carry on, they retired to the hut and watched his antics through the window with mounting amusement. Two hours later the inspector did the only thing he could do and manfully admitted defeat. So they let him into the secret and made a friend for life.

Sam was a most unusual inspector and came from Stafford Road, Wolverhampton. He was short and stocky with a bristling white moustache, so stocky, in fact, that when riding as a passenger in my 1926 Austin Seven, he had difficulty in getting the door shut. He specialised in cranes and out-of-gauge loads, and what he did not know about either was not worth knowing. He would stand for a full five minutes looking at a 10 ton anchor waiting to be loaded on to a 'crocodile'; he would then take from his pocket a piece of chalk and make a mark on the shank.

"Put the chain round there," he would say to the slinger

under the crane. And up would go the anchor, level, steady, and under complete control.

Although I did once persuade Sam to climb up the jib of one of my cranes, in wet weather and wearing his best suit, he was a man who felt that his days of doing manual work were over and he was at his best when telling other people what to do. I was not surprised, therefore, at what happened when Sam went to the Birmingham Railway Carriage and Wagon works at Handsworth to load some coaches for export to Hong Kong. Separated from their wheels, the coaches were to be loaded on flat wagons and held in place by brackets specially fabricated at Swindon. I was working on the out-of-gauge section at Snow Hill at the time when Sam phoned me up to say that the brackets were two inches out and would have to be altered; nor, if the coaches were to catch their ship, was there time to send them back to Swindon.

"Couldn't the Wagon Works help?" I suggested. "They must have got the means of doing anything like that down there."
"Ar," said Sam. "We'll see."

Some two hours later one of the gaffers at the wagon works came on the phone to me.

"I believe," he said, "that you have in your employ a man named Sam?"

"Yes".

"Well, it may interest you to know that he has taken control of our forge and is giving orders right and left. Says you suggested it."

I explained that it was all for our mutual benefit and the story had a happy ending.

Numerous signalman would relate a similar tale. At a time when the 'brass' would visit their patch by train and who were similarly recognised by the staff from their various stations, a quick phone call would ensure no one was caught out. At some locations there was even a local code on the block-bell, 'expect VIP' and meaning there was time for everything to be made ready, the illicit radio hidden and any unauthorised visitors shooed away.

PUBLIC RELATIONS (or is it 'IMAGE'?)

Public relations, except perhaps in what MacDermot calls the 'period of lethargy' prior to the 'awakening of 1888', were always kept well to the fore by the Great Western.

After 1921 it did not need to conceal the fact that it was the best line in the country; the paltry criticisms made by the other companies were only signs of jealousy and petty spite. With such aids as fast and famous expresses, copper bands round engine chimneys, 'Holiday Haunts', and excellent posters, Paddington generated a glamour that, in spite of nationalisation, lasted beyond the end of steam. (Some would say 'And quite right too!')

Much of this was down to the efforts of the men at the top: down at station level there could be problems. Legally, of course, everything had been taken care of. The GWR Rule Book ordained (Rule 2 - ii) that all staff should be 'prompt, civil, and obliging', as well as (Rule 2 - iii) 'neat in appearance'. British Railways repeated the rules word for word. (In passing, it is interesting to note that the same adjectives - prompt, civil, and obliging, - also appear in the Egyptian State Railways' Rule Book for 1908 (Rule 5); but there, perhaps, such lofty ideals of conduct were a little harder to achieve).

As anyone who has ever been in charge of anything knows only too well, it is quite easy to say or write down what ought to happen, but not so easy to see that it is carried out.

How, the stationmasters and goods agents asked themselves, were they to bring about that happy day when their neat staff (preferably with rosy cheeks and buttonholes) were prompt, civil, and obliging to the public? And that public, of course, included those people who asked silly questions, argued at booking office windows, chucked litter and empty beer bottles about the place, or, over at the goods yard, made insulting remarks and parked their cars without permission.

The roots of the conflict went very deep. There were some staff who were so wrapped up in the running of the railway, that they would have been quite happy to exclude the public altogether: it merely, they thought, that the public got in the way and made the running of actual trains more difficult.

One stationmaster used to try to counter this attitude by preaching sermons to his staff along the lines of, "The public may seem like a 'shower' to you, but they are your bread and butter as well". Other staff, being men of spirit and not made of wood, and knowing that they were doing a good job, returned the insults over the net with 10% extra venom added. It was all very fraught.

Meanwhile the public, brought up from childhood to laugh at the railways as a whole, let alone their sandwiches and waiting rooms, felt, reasonably enough, that as it was paying out good money it was entitled to good service. There was no refreshment room at West Bromwich to sell sandwiches, but they certainly had a case where the waiting room was concerned. It was a vast room where, in winter, you could not see the ceiling for freezing smog. The only furniture was a horse hair settee which faced an empty grate, empty that is except for a framed notice that said "Prevention of consumption. Do not spit."

Within the goods department much of the direct contact with the public was over the telephone. At Netherton the duty of answering the phone fell to young Dan, our lad-messenger. Prior to 1 January 1948, he used to say in his inimitable Black Country treble, "Netherton Goods, Great Western. Who d'you want?" But after nationalisation it was laid down from high above that the telephone should be answered with the words, "British Railways - at your service." This, we gathered, was to portray a state industry working devotedly for the public good. For some reason of his own, young Dan was reluctant to say 'at your service' and, after a few days, telephone conversations used to open like this:-

Dan: "British Railways."
Caller: "Haven't you forgotten something, sonny?"
Dan: "Oh yes......at your service."
Caller: "That's better. Is the gaffer in?"

Confronted with the same instruction from Paddington as to how the telephone should be answered, Snow Hill really

went to town. They had been told to furnish a report on the reactions of the public to the, 'British Railways at your service' stuff, and accordingly told the ladies on the telephone exchange to compile one. The ladies took the request as it stood and produced the following statistics:-
Percentage of public Response

10% "Oh how nice!"
20% "I'm glad to hear it."
70% "Good God!"

These figures were received coldly by Paddington who replied saying that this was a serious matter and should not be treated with levity.
The advent of diesel multiple units for local services in Birmingham and the Black Country by the Western Region was heralded by a blaze of publicity. They would be clean, fast, and punctual, the public was told by conceited posters on hoardings. The great day dawned and a more than usually large crowd assembled on the up platform at West Bromwich to admire or travel on this splendid new service. Heads were turned to the right, watching the up line as it curved under the bridge into the station. Ten minutes after the advertised time, round the corner came two scruffy old carriages hauled by an aged 0-6-0 tank engine belching clouds of sulphurous smoke. A stentorian voice rang out from among the waiting passengers.

"I tode yer, day I?" it said.

©Peter Barnfield

BUFFETS AND TRAIN CATERING

Railway catering has come a long way since the days of the compulsory stop at the Swindon Refreshment Rooms. Dining cars, buffet cars, griddle cars, Pullman service, first and second sitting luncheon, tea, at-your-seat-service, all have come and mostly gone - to be replaced by an impersonal trolley service serving beverages of uncertain taste, and little more than salt and calorie bursting snacks.

Where have the days gone when images of main courses ready to be cooked on an anthracite-fed cooker were seen being loaded into the fridges prior to the start of the journey (even if the raw meat was recorded being placed on the shelf above a pre-prepared desert). When silver-service was the norm, and the cutlery and crockery displayed the proud legend of the owning company? Sadly I now realise I was born too late to have enjoyed Huntley & Palmers railway selection of biscuits, or to have partaken of a cooked breakfast served on a London bound express which left the unmistakable aroma of egg and bacon as it passed us schoolboys waiting for own train in 1963. Not surprisingly said train was known to all as, 'the egg and bacon'.

Then there were the station buffets, sandwiches and rolls lined up on plates behind a sloping glass and chrome display, 'egg and tomato' rolls were my personal favourite, never once did I notice the curling edges of its neighbour, the 6d or was it 1/- price considered acceptable at the time. Pasties seemed to be the only other food available, everything served by surly looking waitresses in off-white uniforms and caps to match.

Refreshment rooms were also always so stuffy. One could watch the steam from an ever boiling water heater rising to the ceiling whence it would condense before running down the walls - or was that a crafty means of attempting to ensure the food remained moist in such an atmosphere? If so it was unsuccessful. Tea was served in white cups and saucers, no mugs or polystyrene holders with a plastic stirrer. I have still yet to work out which end you hold and which end you use for actual stirring.

At the larger stations there the invariable licensed refreshment room and restaurant. Research tells me that in the latter category there were once restaurants to suit the different class of passenger - presumably coq-au-vin in one and straightforward chicken in the other. These too have vanished, replaced by fast food outlets, pasty shops, sandwich stalls and of course the High Street chain stores who besides inviting us to purchase magazines and essentials have likewise muscled in on attempting to feed our ever expanding waistlines. (My excuse at least.)

Which brings me to the point of the tale, (which is not to relate how I ended up in hospital with food poisoning back in 1966 subsequently traced to a BR ham sandwich on a Waterloo - Exeter service in 1966). Instead it refers to an occasion twenty plus years later when I was privileged to undertake a short spell of consultancy work on behalf of the Western Region public relations department.

On the 'Western' I was also granted first class travel to the destination, the southern being less benevolent. Whatever, the principal part of the journey was first class from Reading to Cardiff. I forget the exact purpose but it was something to do with new traffic from a nearby steel works or possibly merry-go-round coal to the power station at Aberthaw.

Backtracking slightly, at Reading I settled myself into my seat to be politely asked a few moments later 'If Sir would be partaking of breakfast?' I settled just for toast, which duly arrived - on a china plate - together with two individual wraps of butter. The process of transferring butter to toast with the requisite implement is well known and need not be repeated (if you are unsure I suggest you seek help elsewhere), but in the process and unbeknown to me, a generous dollop of butter had somehow managed to deposit itself on my tie - where it duly remained past Didcot, Swindon, Bristol Parkway and Newport.

The intended impression of the professional was ruined, think I will stick to a polystyrene cup and packet of biscuits in future.

'THE BISCUIT FACTORY'

'A herd of cows grazing in the watermeadows beside the River Bunting provides rich creamy milk for butter, the most important ingredient of Whimshire's famous Bunting Biscuits, the buttermilk feeding seven fine fat pigs guzzling outside the thatched dairy. Hens scratch for corn spilt on its way to the water powered flour mill while eggs are being gathered. A signwriter is nearly toppled from his ladder by a runner bearing samples of the latest batch of bicuits to quality control for tasting while two ginger cats wait hopefully for crumbs. Locomotive Oat brings coal over the weighbridge to heat the ovens and lots of new delicacies are being created in the recipe room.'

AUDITORS

I do not think it would be disrespectful to the shade of the Great Western Railway to say that it was the policy to issue detailed instructions to cover every eventuality, and then employ a fleet of inspectors and others to see that the instructions were carried out to the letter.

This applied equally to things as far apart as a Junction Pilot - that bugbear of those taking the signalling exam - and the correct procedure to be adopted by a station confronted with an incoming invoice with an amount in the 'paid on' column, but not extended to the 'paid' or 'to pay' column. (The answer to that dilemma was not to accept it.) But, as all good pre-war railwaymen will remember, there was one exception to this rule. An invoice with a 'paid on' only for sack risk upon certain railway-owned sacks could be accepted.

The fleet of inspectors covered the whole spectrum of railway work. As well as those concerned with predictable matters such as signaling, there were gentlemen who came from Paddington to check if the wagon return was being correctly compiled. They arrived out of the blue one morning, put a great strain on the office tea club, justly criticised the writing in the lad-numbertaker's note book, and sallied out into the yard to uncover a long list of mistakes.

There were fire prevention inspectors who examined fire buckets, hoses, hydrants, and patent portable squirts; fuel inspectors who criticised gas rings that were left burning to light cigarettes, and tut-tutted at piles of slack in the coal bin.

There were welfare officers who, with pencil and note book at the ready, made a bee line for the staff toilets to find something wrong there. There were other gentlemen who were interested in claims prevention, bonus payments, compilation of paybills, and, when they still existed, the welfare of the horses.

But the most formidable of all these people were the auditors. Selected by, and owing allegiance to, the chief accountant at Paddington, they were not as other men: they were a corps d'elite. They were stern individuals who wore dark overcoats and had a penchant for Anthony Eden hats.

Such men, their station victims felt, were omniscient; where auditors were involved, it was best not to reason why. For obvious reasons the most important element in the auditors' plan of campaign, when making their annual visit to a station, was the element of surprise. If they were going to catch anyone mixing the sand with the sugar, surprise was essential. Thus the first thing they did after entering the door was to ask for the key of the safe where the petty cash was kept.

In a rabbit warren of railways like the Black Country this surprise was not easy to achieve. One morning at Netherton my chief clerk and I were discussing the day's letters and things in general when the phone rang. It was the stationmaster at our nearest passenger station, Windmill End. Four chaps, he said, had got off the train and set off along the canal tow-path in our direction. Though strangers to him, he said, they looked like auditors, Paddington hats and all.

Foolishly perhaps, we decided to have some fun. We took from the safe the petty cash book and the wooden bowl with the money in it and placed them on my desk with the safe key alongside. There was a knock at the door and in filed the four men. It was raining and they were very wet, dripping pools of water on to the floor.

"Good morning," I said, "can I help you?"
"Audit Department." said their chief portentously.
"Help yourself!" I said, pointing to the key, book, and cash bowl.
The chief auditor looked annoyed: very annoyed.
"How did you know...?" he began and then paused. Years spent ticking figures with a green pencil made putting two and two together to make four second nature to an auditor. He began to thaw somewhat.
"I think I begin to see," he said.

One problem auditors encountered at remote industrial or country stations was where to get something to eat or drink. An auditor with a thermos somehow did not look right; definitely not de rigueur. Instead for their morning and afternoon cups of tea they used to join the office tea club, each cup having to be used twice as there were never enough to go round; but their mid-day meal was another matter. (Stations, in those days, had dinners: only divisional and district offices, and Paddington, had lunch.)

Etiquette did not allow them to forgather with any of the station staff at a local pub or cafe; they had to take their custom elsewhere, even if it meant quite a walk.

One stationmaster I knew used to turn this difficulty to his advantage. His station was deep in the country on a single line, with the station house built over the booking and parcels offices. Access to his kitchen was by a flight of steps up from the booking office with a door at the bottom. There being no alternatives, he used to invite the auditor to dinner. I asked him how this worked.

"Splendid," he said. "I watch him while he's checking away, and if he looks like poking his nose into something I don't particularly want him to see, I just open the door to the kitchen stairs and give him a whiff of liver and onions that the wife's cooking upstairs. Then I suggest we break off for dinner. It always works: he's up those stairs like a cat".

An auditor in South Wales went out in the middle of the day and did himself rather too well at the pub round the corner. It was a hot day and, as he sat ticking away with his green pencil, he found it impossible to keep awake. His head slumped forward on to his hands and he slept. The staff working in the same room wisely decided to let sleeping auditors lie; not so a young clerk from one of the offices upstairs. He tip-toed up behind the sleeper and shouted 'Boo' in his ear; then he ran. But he was not quite fast enough. The auditor had just seen the colour of the clerk's jacket as he vanished through the door. With a savage look in his eye, the auditor stretched himself and then set off on a tour of inspection until he found the rest of the jacket whose sleeve he had seen. Next he proceeded to give the work of the clerk inside the jacket a most meticulous going-over, making copious notes of all the mistakes that he found. Discretion would have been the better part of valour.

Though most auditors did their work thoroughly and justly, some of them could be difficult to say the least. One such unearthed what he thought was a deadly sin at Oldbury Goods in the Black Country. To his horror he found that the goods agent was not paying in his revenue cash every day at Langley Green passenger station, some I/- (5p) bus ride away.

The amount of cash involved was negligible as it was only when some unwary coal merchant was caught weighing a load over the railway weighbridge, or using the railway telephone, that they took any actual money at all. The goods agent had been keeping the money in the safe until he had enough to make the trip worthwhile.

When his sins were pointed out to him, the goods agent was incensed.

"If I took the money to Langley every day," he said, "the bus fares would come to more than what I was paying in."
The auditor was not to be moved.
"Have you," he asked icily, "a written authority to relax what you should know are the rules?"
"No".
"Quite" said the auditor.

From 'Behind the Lines' by Christopher Burton.

OPPOSITE NUMBERS

A passenger, a milk churn, and a truck of coal, all had one thing in common: their journeys by rail had a specific beginning and an end. This meant that there had to be railwaymen to look after the start of their journey, while, at the other end, more railwaymen had to be there to see them off the premises. And stations, like people, had characters of their own: some were helpful, some selfish, some arrogant, and some never seemed alive enough to be anything at all.

Thus it was that stations at opposite ends of regular traffic flows soon got to know each other's peculiarities. That is not to say that they ever met each other in the flesh; contact was by correspondence memo, telegram, or telephone. If the people at the other end were helpful, then you were helpful too; if they 'did it on' you then you 'did it on' them in return. Thus Station A, if upset by Station B, would deliberately omit to advise B that the chief inspector was on his way, so depriving them of that advance warning so essential for ensuring that everything was just so in readiness for the great man's arrival. On the other hand, if relations were good, it could work the other way.

In the late 1930s the staff at Swansea High St. worked closely with their opposite numbers at the chain of little stations strung out along the Vale of Neath. There was a train that left Swansea on Saturday nights soon after the pubs had shut and stopped at all stations up the valley. Few people can cause more trouble than a gentleman 'in beer' who has been over-carried late at night beyond his destination, so Swansea took steps to see to it that this did not happen. As the passengers arrived on the platform, some more steadily than others, the staff checked the destinations of likely candidates and stowed them carefully in pre-arranged compartments. After the train had gone, Swansea had a session on the 'bus phone something like this:—

"That you Resolven? Swansea here. Sixbeauties for you, first compartment, second coach."

"That you Glyn Neath? Swansea here. Three beauties for you, second compartment, second coach."

And so on. The little stations up the valley, knowing where to look, saw to it that their particular customers were safely and tactfully detrained.

From 'Behind the Lines'
by Christopher Burton.

'Six beauties for you, first compartment, second coach'.

A good example of interplay with the people at the other end took place between Kidderminster Goods and Leeds. Both stations loaded a wagon to each other almost every day. It was summer and the cricket season had started; Worcestershire were playing Yorkshire at Worcester; and Worcestershire won. This was in the days when Worcestershire were not the great side they later became; a win over Yorkshire was quite something.

The Kidderminster men decided to celebrate the victory by making those Yorkshire supporters eat dirt. And where better than at Leeds? The folding doors of the van being loaded to

Leeds were cleaned down and all old chalk marks removed. In their place, with a piece of fresh new chalk, the full result of the game was carefully inscribed in best copy-book writing, with the word 'WON' in capital letters. No rude comments were added: they felt that the facts were enough by themselves. And away went the wagon northwards.

Presumably licking their wounds, the Yorkshiremen maintained a dignified silence: Kidderminster, who had been hoping for some pleasing reaction, soon forgot about the matter. But that was not the end of the story.

A day or two after the conclusion of the next meeting between the two county sides, which had taken place at Leeds and ended with a handsome win for Yorkshire, I was walking down the goods shed. Loud laughter could be heard coming from a cluster of men grouped round the doors of a covered van they had just opened. On the inside of the doors were inscribed the full details of Yorkshire's win, with the word 'WON' in very large block letters. A porter knelt down and pulled the wagon label from the clip: 'From Leeds to Kidderminster' it said.

There was a certain amount of wicked satisfaction to be obtained from 'doing it on' your opposite numbers by letting them in for awkward situations. This was all very regrettable, no doubt, but only a continuation of that urge a schoolboy feels to place a strategically located drawing pin on the bench of the boy in front while the latter is standing up to recite some poetry.

So it was in 1967. Hockley had been called upon to assist Birmingham's new concentration depot at Curzon St. for all parcels traffic in the city. But as usually happened, the best laid plans of railway planners whilst fine on paper had failed to take account of the age old adage, 'Sods Law'.

As the decks of Curzon St.'s nice new depot vanished under a sea of parcels, and lines of waiting parcels vans had to be stabled outside, something had to be done. Half the inwards traffic was diverted to Hockley. Among the tens of thousands of parcels which flowed out on to Hockley's decks were some very odd things.

In through the gate came some extremely vexed members of the public hunting for things that were missing. There were tomorrow's bridegrooms looking for their wedding suits, actors looking for their costumes, and people who said that their missing parcel should be easy to find as it was done up in brown paper.

Among all the bedlam, a checker came across a gold fish in a plastic bag full of water labelled to an address in Sutton Coldfield. Considering his rather straightened circumstances, the fish seemed remarkably cheerful. He was gently transhipped to a wash-basin while the water in his bag was changed, and he seemed grateful when a kind-hearted crane-driver dropped some bread crumbs into the bag for his dinner. But what were we going to do as we did not want to provide him with over-night accommodation?

Strictly speaking, Sutton Coldfield was in Walsall's delivery area; and, although we had allocated a lorry for Sutton, it had already left and was not due back until late in the afternoon. Just about to leave, however, was the 8 ton lorry which shuttled between us and Walsall carrying ordinary sundries traffic. It took a bit of persuading to get the motor-driver, who was a Walsall man, to co-operate: but he finally left with the fish ensconced on the spare seat in the cab of his Scammell.

We had come off second best in a recent encounter with Walsall, and I looked forward to the phone call which I knew would come from my opposite number. As I thought he might do, he sounded rather aggrieved.

"What", he asked, "am I supposed to do with this damned fish?"
"That's easy, Ken," I said; "do what we did; change his water and send him on his journey."

LIGHT RAILWAYS - 2

'STARTING THE RAILCAR AT VOBLEY MILLS Plumbury Bagotte & Vobley Mere Railway, Whimshire'.

'Because most passenger trains need to reverse at Vobley Mills, which has no loop line, the PB&VMR invested in a railcar. Number 1, there never were a No.2 or any others, was prone to overheating when running in reverse, and then cutting out. Ilia, the Plumbury Bagotte pilot, was often summoned to the rescue but on this occasion a passing traction engine has offered to help, much to the detriment of the wooden cattle grids. The Turp Bros, have been engaged to decorate the station, a task which will no doubt entail painting over the rot!'

'TRIALS WITH THE NEW RAILCAR, Portersfoote Bunting Light Rly.'

'Railcar No 1, on loan to the PBLR from its manufacturers, receives a helping hand from Hyssop as it attempts to negotiate a steep gradient on the branch to Cuttle and Sepia Foliate. After unsuccessful trials the railcar was relegated to the rhubarb siding at Portersfoote Bunting.'

©Peter Barnfield

'OTTEROAKE LANE LEVEL CROSSING Plumbury Bagotte & Vobley Mere Railway, Whimshire'

'Being a very minor station on the PB&VMR, Otteroake Lane is only provided with a grounded narrow-gauge carriage body to serve as passenger accommodation. One sawn off end of this carriage has been converted into a small 'signal box' containing two levers, an armchair and tea making apparatus. The gatekeeper, having left his door ajar, is about to see it demolished by Theophane, pulling smartly away with a passenger train, with a crew who seem much more interested in a couple of passengers than in looking at the way ahead!'

©Peter Barnfield

RETIREMENT

When a railwayman thought about retirement, the picture that came into his mind was of one of those bald or white-headed old nuisances who came to the station at intervals for their free passes and then wandered round wasting people's time. They asked silly questions; told well-worn anecdotes; and exuded a critical air of things-ain't-what-they-used-to-be. Only when he was past fifty-five did he begin to imagine himself in the same role.

Even so, retirement had been with him since the day when, a spotty junior in his first month of service, he had had a grubby piece of foolscap placed in front of him by the chief clerk, foreman, or secretary of the L.D.C. A compelling voice had then told him that 'Old Sid finishes on Friday, and would he like to subscribe? 'Too shy to ask who Old Sid was, he had meekly added his name among the ls.(5p) small fry at the bottom of the list. Above his name, starting at the top with a pound from the gaffer, the signatures of his workmates had descended in strict order of seniority and pecuniary generosity.

Railway conservatism being what it was, few changes were ever made in the ritual of retirement. Thus the next part of the ceremony was the presentation. All staff, except perhaps one to watch the telephone, assembled in the gaffer's office where a shortage of chairs meant that most remained standing and acted as a salutary spur to brevity. Pushed up to the front was the victim; on the gaffer's desk was the clock. The gaffer, batting first, had the pick of the words of praise for the departing. Then others - 'On behalf of the accounts department,' On behalf of the outside staff and so on, struggled with increasing difficulty to think of something nice to say that nobody had said before.

But not always so. Once, in South Wales, I attended the presentation to a retiring chief clerk of the district office. The usual pealing anthems had been swelling the notes of praise when one speaker, batting about fifth, said that he was delighted that Mr. So-and-so was going as he had always found him a most difficult man to deal with, and the office would be a much happier place without him. In the silence that followed this stark statement of the truth, you could hear the presentation clock ticking.

Away from the exception and back to the rule, after the 'victim' had spoken his few halting words of thanks, he was expected to take his friends 'round the corner' or 'across the road' as local geography required. This part of the ceremony, much of it in working hours, and much of the beer being paid for by someone else, was very well attended indeed. It ended with the victim, now sadly befuddled and financially skint, but still clutching his clock, being taken home at closing time in the cab of a *cartage* vehicle. And that was that.

One staff clerk at Snow Hill had other ideas. He was not, he said, going to buy beer for all his friends at once; this would prevent him saying his goodbyes and thank-yous properly. He would deal with each one individually. So, starting promptly at opening time in the morning of his last working day, he selected his first friend and took him 'down the dive'. They each bought two pints and then the staff clerk returned upstairs to collect his next jolly old pal; another two pints each, and so on throughout the morning. Although he was persuaded later on to change gear from pints to halves, by one o'clock the staff clerk could be seen tacking down the corridor in search of his next victim. By two o'clock he was on his way home in the cab of a parcels van.

British Rail, without disturbing the local traditions of retirement, added (as they did with a lot of other things) another layer to the process. It would be nice and paternal, they felt, for departing staff to be seen by the divisional or district gaffers personally and thanked along with some suitable valedictory remarks. These dismal functions, including cold tea and dull biscuits, were only enlivened when the big gaffer got the names mixed up due to careless work by the staff clerk at his elbow. "Well, goodbye George," he would say genially as if he had known the man all his life, whereas in reality they had never seen each other before, and how is Mrs. Jones going to manage with you at home all of the time?"

"She won't have to," was the reply, "as I'm John Smith. This is Shunter Jones stood next to me."

From 'Behind the Lines' by
Christopher Burton.

...'still clutching his clock...'

Also handed out on these occasions were the "Well-done-thou-good-and-faithful-servant" cards which recorded years of service and stereotyped thanks from the Very Important Person who had probably signed the cards in blank several weeks before, several dozen at a time. These cards are printed on stiff cartridge paper: what exactly the recipient is supposed to do with them has never been quite clear. I have never yet seen one on display.

One attitude towards them was that of one of my West Bromwich motor-drivers. I met him in the yard on his way back from his 'valedictory' in Wolverhampton and noticed that he was not carrying the usual large envelope that should have housed his card.

"Charlie," I said, "didn't they give you a card?"

"Ar," he said.

"Well you must have left it in the train."

His reply was to extract from his waistcoat pocket, where he normally stored cigarette stubs, an already sadly soiled document folded four times. He straightened it out against the side of a wagon and eyed it sourly.

"You can't pay the coalman with that," he said.

A STING IN THE TAIL

Dogs have featured only in passing in previous pages, so it is well overdue that a final account of one particular canine should appear. Collecting dogs, security dogs, even dogs for rounding up sheep and herding these same sheep away from the track might have been considered. The uses of all of these are well known, so instead we will turn our attention to just one, unique animal, in the north east of the LNER and from a station on the fringe of a rural area where the line in question was surrounded with industrial and urban development just a short distance further on. I should warn the reader now there is no happy ending, a happy middle – yes, but subject to this condition, please continued.

Our station was for the most part quiet. A rural outpost consisting of up and down lines plus a small yard on the up side. From here it was primarily farm produce that was transported, coal for domestic purposes received, plus the occasional few trucks of goods intended for the neighbouring urban location but where physical space was often limited. Hence rather than take the vehicles back to the marshalling yard it became the practice to transport it a few miles further on, where there was room and they might then be conveniently placed to be worked back to the intended destination as soon as it was convenient.

Save for the name and paintwork, our station was typical of hundreds of others, a station master (junior grade), clerk, three porters, one early and one late turn, plus an additional man graded as a porter signalman. This man would cover for two hours during the day between the early turn signalman finishing and the late turn man – who worked 4.00 pm to midnight - coming on duty. Due to having plenty of space, the location was also home to the local p/way gang, although apart from when they might be working in the immediate area, these men would arrive daily and often not be seen again until finishing time. Finally there was the lad-porter, we may call him Frank, not his real name, who worked a day shift thus coming into contact with the complete staff on a regular basis.

At this stage I should mention the origins of this tale. A man, whom I have never met in person, but who has assisted in other books with images from his youth taken in the south of England, recounted to me this story as had been told to him. Said photographer is now domicile not far from where what will be related occurred. It is not a shaggy-dog story in the sense of the word but one which in its time became so unique it was still being spoken of in the various local public houses years later – hence our photographer picking up the gist. Allowing then for the inevitable colouring that occurs with age…..

In 1934 our lad, Frank, turned 15. His home was smallholding high on the hills above the railway. In the distance could be seen the outline of smoking chimney and gantry cranes on the Tyne away to the east, but for Frank at least live was more peaceful, a rural idyll. Some might consider his to have been a lonely existence, an only child, he had no particular interests, save a love of animals of which there were a limited number on the smallholding. Amongst these was the farm dog, of doubtful parentage, she could never be considered to be one of breeding, but caught in the correct light and at the right angle there was a definite lineage visible.

Having left school Frank had to turn his attention to a working life from now on, ideally he would have preferred to stay on the farm, but times were hard and what could be made from long hours and hard work was only just sufficient to support the small family, certainly not the wages of an additional hand. Hence Frank found himself helping out for nothing, that is until one day his father made an announcement – well two actually. "Just to let you know, vet says the dogs going to have pups, don't know how, but I did see a stray sniffing around t'while back……" He continued, "You might wants to get yourself down the station as well, I was down there with the feed t'other day and I hears they be looking for a lad. Good work that on the railway, more than you could get here."

As this is a story relating to a dog and not the means of recruitment on the LNER in the 1930s, suffice to say Frank dutifully attended, convinced those with the authority to make a decision he was the best applicant and shortly after started work.

The term 'Lad porter' was also a misnomer, for he was expected to do exactly the same work as the adults, although naturally for less pay – as a 'lad'. Because he came from a framing background and with it the strength to control young bullocks and the like, heavy sacks or tarpaulins posed no problem and he was soon accepted as a valuable member of the station 'family'.

"You continue as you are and in a couple of years you could apply for a better job up the line." Were the regular words of encouragement he would receive from the station master. Frank would touch his cap and reply with a simple, "Yessir", but in heart he had no intentions of moving, the thought of life away from the countryside he knew had no appeal. Besides there was something much more attractive at home.

'Mum' had given birth to a litter of five, as puppies all of course delightful but Frank had asked to keep one and he and pup, a female which for reasons that are unknown he called 'M', had quickly become inseparable.

For the first few weeks of course puppies and mum were together, but sharp young teeth meant mother was quickly keen for them to become independent as regards nourishment after which they would only return to her for comfort and at night. Around eight weeks the other four disappeared to new homes, leaving mum and pup to have the run of the area.

As mentioned though, Frank and the pup had already formed a bond, so it was no real surprise one day when aged about four months pup squeezed its way under the fence by the gate and instead of sitting dolefully as Frank set off to work, she followed, a happy wagging tail showing she was determined not to be separated any more.

To Frank, M was far more important than work, it mattered not what the regulations might say – whether they did or not was not important – he just marched straight to the door of the station master's office, knocked and almost presented a statement that his dog had come with him, she would not get in the way, and he would look after her not to the detriment of his work.

In reality I suspect the station master kept a wary eye, but he need not have bothered, that unwritten bond that was already there was growing stringer all the time, so whilst M might wander slightly to investigate smells, sights and sounds, the rest of time she was either at Frank's side or keeping him in sight - the latter if he had instructed her to 'wait' whilst engaged in shunting or some other potentially hazardous activity was taking place.

Partly due to Frank's own popularity, so M too became well liked. The men would share titbits with her, the station master regularly brought his children to see her, and passengers would enquire after her welfare.

In appearance she was brown with short hair, about the size of a retriever but with a head of a different shape. Rarely did she bark, about the only time when a stranger might appear in the yard and this only to alert Frank.

She could also almost sense when a train was due, did she hear the signal wires being pulled or recognise the signals in a different position, we cannot know. Whatever, she would wait away from the rails, only venturing forward to cross the track when all was again quiet and then when called to do so.

The only place she would not visit was the signal box. The operating floor accessed by a set of wooden steps having open treads, probably the latter holding some fear about loosing her balance.

I mentioned earlier how passengers might enquire after her, this was commonplace if she lay watching Frank at work on the actual platform whilst a train stood prior to departure. Collecting tickets almost became a nightmare, those arriving wanting to mill around to pat and pet, stern faced men and tired looking women finding the time to pause awhile, M enjoying the moment, at the same time throwing her head back as if to say "Don't stop".

She also had her uses, a dropped scarf or hat was quickly retrieved whilst rats were now infrequent visitors to the goods shed. Obviously not as quick or nimble as a terrier at such a task, she nevertheless made a good impression, to the detriment of the rat population and the applause of the traders whose hessian sacks had previously all too often shown the signs of disturbance.

One thing Frank had been wary from the start was when the occasional visit by an Inspector might take place, but he need not have worried. Possibly words were said beforehand, as nothing was ever mentioned save for the fact that, "Frank there is a vacancy at so and so that would suit you, shall I put your name forward, more money but you would have to lodge and you won't be able to take M with you."

In his heart Frank knew that eventually he would be forced to move, after all he had been a 'lad' for five years now, but it was the thought of leaving 'M' that made the decision impossible for him.

Sadly nature would take a hand in that decision. One morning in the glorious summer of 1939 Frank came downstairs to find M in her basket instead of waiting to greet him. She seemed reluctant to follow that morning whilst also having a slight cough and a limp on one leg. Forsaking work, Frank took the pony and trap and made a trip to the vet. "Probably a strain, she will be alright in a couple of days", said the vet, the cough seemingly ignored or not mentioned.

Daily trips to the vet followed, Frank ignoring work content just to nurse his friend who had given him such love in the past and who was visibly sinking fast. Now it was his turn to respond with kindness.

Notwithstanding everything available to the vet, M continued to deteriorate. She was a young dog, five is no age, and the thought of her not recovering was something he could not contemplate.

Less than a week later, Frank was told there was nothing more to be done. Watching his beloved M lying on the table was the hardest thing he had ever had to do, she died in his arms, surrounded by his tears.

For some months, Frank would not talk of the experience, family and friends suggested he must get another dog, not another 'M' but a new friend. As it was elsewhere in the world tears were being shed all over. The events of 1939 are too well known to need repeating here, suffice to say Frank was amongst the first to volunteer, sadly he would also be one of the first to fall.

Frank's remains were eventually returned to his home, where on a hillside overlooking what had once been the local station he was interred alongside the ashes of his beloved 'M'.

To persist along the same lines as previous, the reader might care to seek out a copy of

'The Railways of Rockall'

by Dr Ing and Professor F W Hampson, published in 1990 (ISBN 0-9516697-0-2).

In this seminal work the authors explore the use of the gyroscopic principal as applied to rail vehicles when exposed to extreme conditions of wind. Drawings of such vehicles are included.

There is also a photograph of locomotives and rolling held 'in reserve' deep within a tunnel.

Unfortunately it was taken without the benefit of flash.